Keep dancing

Carmen

Dancing Naked...
in fuzzy red slippers

Carmen Richardson Rutlen

Cypress House

Dancing Naked ... in fuzzy red slippers

Cypress House
155 Cypress Street
Fort Bragg, CA 95437
(800) 7737782
www.cypresshouse.com

Front cover design and illustration by Mike English
Book production by Cypress House

Library of Congress Cataloging-in-Publication Data
Rutlen, Carmen Richardson, 1948-
Dancing naked-- in fuzzy red slippers /
by Carmen Richardson Rutlen.--
1st ed.
p. cm.
ISBN 1-87938453-1 (alk. paper)
1. Self-actualization (Psychology) 2. Conduct of life.
I. Title.
BF637.S4R877 2003
158--dc21   2003004850

Printed in the USA
4 6 8 9 7 5

For Dad, who called me Princess and Cowgirl.
And I believed him.

And Mom, who taught me how to give my all
to the dance.

And Toby, who taught me to love with my
heart wide open.

ACKNOWLEDGMENTS

Writing this book has been the most satisfying and soul-wrenching thing I have ever done. Its birth has been long and difficult. I could not have gone through it without the help of the many midwives and midhusbands who assisted me. They stood by my side, telling me when to breathe and when to push, and to hang in there, it would be over soon. They lied—it wasn't over soon. But now that this baby is out, I want to thank you all from the bottom of my heart.

First, I want to thank my sister, Pixie Christiansen (who calls herself Maria), for being a bright and clear light in my life, and whose support and encouragement have given me the courage to climb over treacherous mountains of self-doubt. She has not wavered in her belief in this book, and is an angel of the highest order. I want to acknowledge her wonderful and extremely handsome husband, David, and beautiful children, Dominee (who's an absolute doll) and Tyler (whom I call "Burger Boy"). Thanks to my brother, Johnny Richardson (who calls himself Juan), with a heart as big as all outdoors and who, Pixie and I agree, starts all the family Christmas fights. And his sweet wife, Marilyn, who is like a sister to me, and their beautiful fifteen-year-old daughter, Jill, who, much to her chagrin, Johnny still refers to as "The Baby."

I thank Toby, my incredible son, who is the most creative person I know and helped me come up with the title of this book.

Toby adds beautiful new textures to my life, and is a brilliant musician, hip-hop artist, songwriter, and producer of amazing music. I give heartfelt thanks to Mom, a beautiful dancer, who taught me how to dance to the rhythm of my own heart and who is the unconditional *maestra* for unconditional love. Dad, who died in 1981, is the wisest man I've had the pleasure to know. Dad once told me he was very proud of his children, and when I asked him why, he replied, "Because you've never been in jail." I told him I thought his standards were a little low. I hope he's even more proud now as he lives in this book and in the hearts of everyone who's ever known him.

A warm thank you to Heather McNamara, Editor-in-Chief of *Chicken Soup for the Soul.* She was the first to publish my work in *A 5th Portion of Chicken Soup for the Soul* and two additional pieces in later editions, which provided me the impetus to go forward with the publishing of *Dancing....* I will forever be grateful to Heather. I'd also like to thank Dr. Richard Lederer, who took time out of his busy schedule to read sample pages of an unknown book by an unknown author to whom he gave a glowing review.

Karyn Redburn, a friend in the purest sense, has been there for me as a sounding board for my writing, a sales and marketing maven, and always available with encouraging words and support when I needed them. I'd like to thank Mike English, a brilliant art director, long-time friend, and the genius who created the front cover design. There are no words to convey the height of his talents and the beauty of his heart.

My sincere thanks to all my friends and the people in my network survey group for laboring through my manuscript in its infancy and giving me their insights, support, and candid opinions. Debbie Rutlen, my niece by marriage, whom I kept after my divorce; Leslie Jones, who is writing a delightful children's book; Kathy Amidi-rad, my dear confidante and close friend; Lillian Scoyen, a southern gentlewoman and one of the sweetest, most gracious people I know; Paul Schraub, a dear friend and phenomenally-talented photographer who makes magic happen with a camera; Jazmine White, my wonderful cousin; Larry Cohen, a sidesplitting comedian; Elaine and Vern Rutlen, my ex-in-laws, whom I also kept after my divorce; Steve Rutlen, my past husband, present friend, and good sport; Patsy Rotolo, a talented playwright who will be taking Hollywood by storm with her soon-to-be-released screenplay; Judy Heckerman, who gave my writing such high marks and wonderful comments that, whenever I felt discouraged, I'd pull out her survey sheet and read it over and over; Glen Gray, a close friend who beat all the odds and of whom I am so proud; Joanne Harris, a long-time friend and one of the dearest people I know; Don Sirathhhhh, author of the best-selling *Conquering Cold-Calling Fear* (and whose name is actually spelled S-u-r-a-t-h. He misspelled my name in his book. Don, this is payback.); Andi Gibb, a gifted writer, Beth Townsend, Jeannine Christiansen, Conrad Sanford, Stan Harris, a playwright and ad guy, Alicia Roberts; Sue Butti, another dear longtime friend; Angelo Butti (Sue's sexy Italian hunk of a father-in-law); Will White, who was encouraging at the onset; Donna Sangwin, an ex-client, present friend, and new mother; Judy Biondolillo; Mary Ann Curtis; Candace Baker; a fabulous photographer; Linda Hanleigh; Len De Paolo, a great counselor who helps me find sanity when it's missing; Laura Howard, Katy Weibel, one of Toby's friends who slipped into my heart, too; Barbara Eastman; K. C. Knapp, who is still trying to learn how to drive his yacht; Elaine Preston; Dr. Michelle Indianer, a friend and accomplished psychiatrist to whom I send all my friends; Chris Keeley, Sharon Van Wingerden, who loves to dance as much as I do; Susan Silver, my sweet supportive friend "Suzie-Q"; Joe, Carol, and Christina of Dolce Spazio; Sue Tuttle, the first person to offer me money for my book; Carol Rutlen, whom I kept after her divorce from my ex-husband; Rick Tharp of Tharp Did It; and Joel Roberts, who taught me how to give a good interview on *The Today Show.*

My acknowledgments would not be complete without mentioning the fine folks at Café Marcella. This restaurant has been to me as the Moulin Rouge was to Toulouse-Lautrec. It's where I did a lot of writing and a fair amount of inspirational drinking. I'd like to thank all my friends at Café Marcella: Alain, the handsome French owner and his lovely wife Martine; Larry, the manager and former English professor who assisted me with composition and syntax and will one day publish his 300 pages of poetry that lie in his closet; my buddies Dave, Mark, and Todd, beautiful guys inside and out, who always let me sit at a four-top so I could spread out and write; Nicholas, a newlywed who wears that newlywed glow; Brian; Danny; Matthew; Vincente and Nick, the fabulous Italian chef. Café Marcella has the best food in the world served by the nicest people in the world.

My sincere thanks to my publisher, Cynthia Frank of Cypress House, for putting up with my endless questions and countless changes, and Joe Shaw, my brilliant editor with whom I screamed, fussed, and argued and who made me write English good. And who, through it all, made me a better writer.

Lastly, I'd like to thank every person who's stumbled into my life, including the teenage girl who took my parking space at the mall that Christmas; the trucker who flipped me off for cutting in front of him (I didn't see you!); the dates I had who never called back, and the ones who did; the clients who hired me; the clients who didn't; the people who hurt me; the people who loved me. Each and every one of you had a message for me. You are all reflected in this book and have helped in my ongoing process of self-discovery. You have all played your parts marvelously well. And, hopefully, I have played my part well for you. You have all made this book and my life possible and always a grand adventure.

And if I've forgotten someone, I'll catch you on the next book.

Contents

Chapter 1

FANDANGO ~ FAMILY AND FRIENDS

The fandango of family and friends is a dance full of lively rhythms. This is a dance with people we love, and sometimes, don't. Family is given to us, friends we choose. Some we keep forever, others we lose along the way, but each and every one of them splashes our lives with bold, masterful strokes of color. And when we rise above and look from a distance, we can view this spectacular dance in a rainbow of colors we call ... family and friends.

THE BUG

I noticed a bug
in my glass of water today.
I drank it
to see if I would die.

I didn't.

I think I will start testing
other things
Mom said were true
that might not be.

PARENTS

Parents are
people who believe in you,
for no actual reason.

FRIENDS

Friends are
people you love,
that you don't have to.

THE ENEMY

I used to see women as the enemy. Maybe it was because they saw
me as the enemy. If a girl didn't like me, Mom said it was because
she was jealous. I think all moms tell their daughters that.

Now, some of the dearest people I know are women. They
comfort me. We share similar sorrows, similar joys. I'm glad I
have finally let women into my life. And I guess they were never
jealous — or I got ugly.

SINGLE WORKING MOTHER

As a single working mother
I didn't have time
to be successful and neat.
I gave up neat.

STUPID

My fifteen-year-old son
thinks I'm stupid.

I depend on that.

I can move stealthily through his life
in an ambush mode,
moving about freely,
as my cleverest maneuvers
look stupid to him.

JUSTICE

I had a friend who,
every time she touched something
with her right hand,
would have to touch it
with her left hand too,
to make it even.

It took her longer to do things,
but I admired
her sense of justice.

3

OXYGEN

When I used to sit on an airplane, waiting for takeoff, I was always surprised and frankly horrified as the flight attendant presented her canned speech, while she pointed out the exits with arms moving in cheerleader-like precision, explaining how we could save ourselves if the plane were to fall from the sky.

What horrified me was not the thought of free falling from the sky, but rather the instructions given to mothers that in case of a drop in cabin pressure they were to put the oxygen masks on themselves first. Then and only then were they to put the masks on their children. It seemed so wrong, so cold, so selfish — really bad.

Then, I had a baby. The baby grew into a child. I discovered that extreme mothering could lead to oxygen deprivation for the mother. Devoting every moment of every day to fulfilling my child's slightest needs, wants, and whims became not only exhausting but also caused me oxygen starvation. I couldn't breathe.

One inspired day I came up for oxygen. I signed up for a watercolor class, two hours every Thursday night. One night a week of being unequivocally, self-lovingly, me. Not a mother, not an employee, not anybody's girlfriend, just me.

Ahh ... the oxygen that came pouring through. That pure, clean, fresh oxygen allowed me to breathe, deeply. As I began to breathe deeper I noticed my son was breathing deeper too, as was my boyfriend and, it seemed, everyone around me.

I now take an oxygen break regularly, without guilt or a second thought, happy that in doing so I am showing my son and everyone who used to depend on me how to take in their own oxygen and breathe, deeply.

RUFUS

(Published in *A 5th Portion of Chicken Soup for the Soul.*)

We had a basset hound named Rufus. We called him the "ding-dong boy." I don't know why. He was a very, very sweet soul. He never bit man or beast. When the vet cut his toenails too short, making them bleed, he would cry and lick the vet. Mean dogs befriended Rufus and turned nice in his presence. Someone once told me that if the dog world had a Jesus Christ, it was Rufus.

Rufus died yesterday. He was fourteen.

I went for a walk in the park today. The world felt different. Changed. There was one less sweet soul. There was a missing piece of the puzzle. It wasn't just my world that was different, it was the whole world, everyone's world. People I passed were unaware of the change. They looked so centered, so normal. They didn't know the world had changed. I felt so small and alone in the knowing.

When I tell my clients that I wasn't in the office yesterday because my dog died, it will sound small, insignificant. Everyone has a dog die at some point. But somehow it feels like no one ever has or ever will feel … what I feel today.

Someone once said that love feels like a kind of exclusivity. Maybe that's what it is. Maybe what I'm feeling is love. It feels like I have an aura that's radiating shades of blue, and there's a red lightning bolt running through the light blue part, clear to the center of my being.

I love you, Rufus, and bless you, and send you, somewhat reluctantly, to your new adventure, hoping it is filled with fields of green grass, chew-bones, all the treats you can eat, and strong legs without arthritis to run in the green fields.

THE ESSAY

When I was in college, I wrote an essay on the word "fuck."

I proudly sauntered into my dad's study and handed him my essay with the large red "A" scribbled on the top. As he read, I awaited the "I'm-so-proud-of-you" accolades sure to come.

Dad's face changed slowly and steadily to a glowing red. In his gruffest, retired-colonel-from-the-army voice he said, and I quote him exactly, "I send my daughter to fucking college and my fucking daughter writes a fucking essay on the word 'fuck' and gets a fucking 'A!'"

In my calmest, I'm-going-to-college-now-and-you can't-talk-to-me-like-a-child voice, I explained Hiakawa's theory of semantics, whereby a word is just a representation of a thing, but is not the thing, much like a map represents the territory but is not the territory. And if indeed words could be bad then words like "murder," "rape," and "kill" would be bad words, not a word that represents making love, like "fuck."

We volleyed words back and forth until our steam ran out. His anger, my self-righteousness, subsided. He then calmly explained, "The purpose of words is to communicate. If you're communicating with a little old lady and use the word 'fuck,' she would consider you an ill-bred young woman and immediately tune you out. Any words that followed would fall on deaf ears. Communication would cease. The very reason for words would cease to exist." He made sense.

What I learned from Dad that day has served me better than Hiakawa's theory ever would. In our lives we are exposed to various forms of truth and "how things should be." Some of these truths we are taught in college. They're fun to theorize about and to know. However, in society, we are an integral part of today's world and today's people, and must at least appear to accommodate the social "truths of the day." And so, there are two sets of truth: one for your heart and soul, the other for the world at large.

And sometimes, on special days, we might be lucky enough to have both sets of truth blend for just a moment, as we say the word "fuck" to a wise little old lady, and she knowingly smiles and then laughs.

EXTENSION

Having a child
is like having
an extension of yourself
that you have no control over.

Like your own arm
gone wild.

WAITING FOR "THE PIX" AT THE RAILROAD STATION

Lonely, stretching railroad tracks. Desolate. Visited only by a stray breeze. A few scattered people waiting, two alone, two together. Waiting. It looks odd, like a smile with teeth missing.

A lone train whistle sounds, of course, in the distance. Thinking about The Pix. Pixie with beautiful long flaxen hair. (What is flaxen, anyway?) Pixie, now the grownup, Maria, my little sister, who is like a big sister to me. Whom I ignored, and indeed don't even remember when she was little. Blank memories.

But not for her. She remembers. She remembers the shunning. She remembers watching me put on makeup for a date. She remembers me yelling at Mom to make her go away. She goes away.

She remembers. My dear little sister. I was a teenager. She was a pesky little sister.

I wonder now how I could have ignored this unignorable, incredible creature. She is rich and strong, wiser than her time. She doesn't know. She handles me better than anyone. Says the exact thing I need to hear at the exact time I need to hear it. She doesn't know. She is a glorious combination of male and female, blending into a beautiful, strong woman. She doesn't know.

If she were a flower she would be an African daisy, strong and true, pointing straight to the sun brazenly, without fear, without shame. Long flaxen hair (I looked it up — it means straw colored. I thought it meant brown. Anyway...), shining, tossing, always moving. Beautiful woman. She doesn't know.

I love her. And I need a word bigger than "love" to define it. And she has learned to put on makeup beautifully, without having had anyone to watch.

Where is that damn train?

Dad Used to Say:

"If you have a complaint, always go to the top guy."
It works in returning an out-of-season dress to Macy's.
And with God.
~

As a child I hated meat loaf. When I threw a hissy fit at the table, not wanting to eat my meat loaf, Dad would say, "You don't have to like it. You just have to eat it."
As I grew up, I realized he was talking about more than just meat loaf. It was useful advice. It has served me well with bosses I didn't like, homework I didn't want to do, duties I didn't want to perform.
However, to this day, I don't eat meat loaf. Because I don't like it and because I don't have to.
~

It's not that I don't like work.
It just takes so much time out of my day.
~

The objective in the game of life
is to minimize the lows,
maximize the highs,
and try not to stay
in the middle too long.
~

When Dad married Mom, she had buckteeth. She was in the process of getting them straightened, when she told my father that she was embarrassed to smile. He said, "Just think, honey, you're one of the few people who can eat corn on the cob through a picket fence." (Nice going, Dad.)

SPARKLE

Most of the time I like myself pretty well, except when I'm feeling
confused
stupid
mean
lazy
wrong.

Most of the time I feel like a little sparkle in everyone's life. However, I wish I felt more like a sparkle in my son's life. It's not for want of trying. I just don't feel like I know how. I try everything to see if anything will work. Sometimes I'm afraid I'll run out of things to try.

Maybe, just maybe, I'm not supposed to sparkle to him at his age. Maybe he needs to find his own sparkle. And perhaps he needs to block out mine … so he can see his own.

GRANDMA

I once saw my grandmother putting on lipstick
without a mirror.
I asked her how she could do that.
She said,
"Honey, if I don't know where my lips are by now,
I guess I never will."

A BOY

I knew a boy who used to get in trouble at school. Interestingly, outside, around his bedroom, there grew big, wild, beautiful flowers, and all the animals in the neighborhood loved him, even the mean dogs. Civilization was not his friend. The big, wild, beautiful things, however, loved him immensely.

I learned to love him like the wild things did. And when I did, I felt a love so large and pure, it made all other forms of love seem so very little.

My son.

DEBBIE

Her mother died when she was three. Her mother's name was Sarah. Debbie had an insatiable hunger for information about her mom, from anyone who had known her or who had even just talked to her. Her hunger embarrassed her, so she held it delicately to the side, not wanting anyone to see too much of it at one time.

She tried asking her grandmother what her mother was like, but her grandmother was a bit nuts and never really answered her. When her grandmother died she felt like she had been holding on to the end of a rope and the rope had shaken her loose, and she was falling.

Then, one day — I'm sure it was bright and sunny — she found another rope and grabbed hold of it. The rope was effortless to hold on to. It felt soft and fit her hands just right. She had a sense of floating. It was her own rope, made of silk and laced with beautiful colors, which was her, and intricately woven with golden threads, which was her mother.

Sarah had, after all, never been very far.

THE CRAZIES

My grandfather, Juan Barcia y Zanuy,
used to tell my mother,
before she left the house,
"Be careful, my daughter,
not all the crazies are locked
in the nut-house."

CUBBYHOLES

Dad used to say, "When you first meet someone you put them in a little cubbyhole, a nice, neat little slot. Then, when you know them a little better, they don't quite fit, so you move them into another cubbyhole. This keeps happening until you know them very well and discover they don't fit into a cubbyhole. Finally, you create a custom cubbyhole just for them."

It's a beautiful sight to see a life filled with custom cubbyholes.

STANDING IN LINE

Mom used to tell me, "When you're standing in a long line, like at the movies, don't just stand facing all the people in front of you, turn around and look at all the people behind you. You'll feel better."

She was right. It's important to see where you've been, not just where you want to go.

Chaos

The ancient Greeks' definition of the word "chaos" referred to the exact moment when sperm and egg meet. I had a baby. The Greeks were correct. Chaos.

"Chaos" also references a moment when nothing is strictly defined and all potentiality exists—all joy, all sorrow, all delight. Again the Greeks were correct. Children and the accompanying chaos make life not only possible, but supremely interesting, and on good days, absolutely delightful. Smart, those Greeks.

Mom Gone Missing

Once, I thought Mom was in danger. She was missing. While I was frantically looking for her, I imagined her gone.

I realized that I'd never written a poem about her, never told her the specific details of how I loved her. Why I loved her. What made her special. How alone I felt when I thought she was gone. How I imagined what it would feel like to not have a "mom" anymore. And how, at last, I would have to be an adult, at forty-eight. How my brother and sister would have to be adults too.

How my son and his cousins would feel, now knowing that people really do die. And how, if they had known, would have been nicer to Abuelita. Would have sat more still when she told them of her experiences in the war, which she called "adventures," as a Spaniard in the Philippines during the Japanese occupation.

Did she know how much I loved her? How, when I was mean to her, I didn't really mean it? How much of her heart had become my heart? How, when my brother or sister teased me about being, "just like Mom," I learned to take it as a compliment?

Well, I found Mom. She'd gotten lost across town and stopped at a house to ask for directions. The young couple invited her in and they spent the day drinking wine.

Mom always says, "if I die," not "when I die." But I'm writing this now just in case, one day, Mom, you're missing ... or hopefully, just drinking wine with strangers.

MARY

I was sad one day.
I told Mary that it felt
like there was a crack in my crust
and I was leaking out.

She said that was good,
because I was filled with sweet berries,
and everyone likes berry juice.

KIM

I came to their house to do a photo shoot for a catalog. As I walked in their home I saw they had the life I wanted. The home was beautiful. The decor was beautiful. The life was beautiful.

He had a prestigious job with a prestigious company. She had a gracious life with time to paint, time to play tennis, and time to tend to her garden. In my mind's eye, I could see her carrying cut roses from her garden in her wicker flower basket. A Martha Stewart lifestyle. A life resplendent with grace and harmony. Reserved, elegant beauty. Their home sat overlooking a golf course. In the backyard, a fountain splashed droplets of water into a blue-tiled spa. Roses in pink and red dotted the perimeter of the graceful wrought-iron fence. It was the kind of house I had dreamed of. It was the life I wanted. The life I longed for. It was a sweet life.

After the photo shoot they asked me to join them on the patio for a gin and tonic. As I sat outside enjoying the sweet smells of summer and the sounds of twittering night birds, they told

13

me about Kim. She had died the previous year. This day would have been her birthday. She would have been twenty-six. She was their only child. They talked of wishes that would never come true. They talked about if there had been grandchildren. They had recently moved to this new home, giving up their grander estate. They could no longer look at their tennis courts where father and daughter had practiced for tournaments. And won some. We talked of Kim. Bright, pretty, precocious, effervescent Kim.

I thought of my home in the suburbs, of my ugly yellow kitchen cabinets, with a floor that didn't match and was usually coated with patches of Popsicle stickiness. The commotion of dogs, cats, a screeching parrot, and neighborhood kids tracking in mud as they stopped in for a fudge bar. And the constant driving beat of loud heavy-metal music blasting from my son's bedroom. I thought about my messy life and the feelings of messy joy it brought. The problems I was having with my nineteen-year-old son suddenly seemed small. Toby had brought home a puppy that was part wolf. I had told him time and time again, "No more animals!" I told him in no uncertain terms to find a home for the puppy. I knew he was sneaking the pup into his bedroom after I had gone to bed. We hadn't spoken for three days. I decided when I got home that night, I would tell him he could keep the puppy.

As we sat outside drinking gin and tonics on that warm summer evening, they showed me photographs of Kim, and I had the sense of a cocoon transformed into a butterfly. I felt a presence like a waft of smoke, which had a subtly recognizable form.

They spoke of dreams in which Kim had come to them. In dreams, she spoke sweetly to her mother. In dreams, she spoke sweetly to her father. She spoke to each of them in different dreaming ways, but always delivering sweet messages of happiness to both. She permeated their home.

And when I left, the cold steel moon was full as I felt a butterfly's wing softly brush against my cheek.

FRIENDSHIP

When a friendship dies,
there's
no right,
no wrong.
Just a soft fizzling out.

Different directions,
different rhythms,
no longer resonating
to the same beat.

And yet,
for every friendship
that has ended,
I am thankful
to have danced
those dances
to the rhythm of those days
when we were
so beautifully
in sync.

THE BOY WITH THE SOFT HEART

When he was a little boy, another little boy told him he had a soft heart. This was in no way meant as a compliment.

As he grew into a man he tried a multitude of ways to hide his soft heart. Whatever he tried, she could see it anyway. Through the years she watched him using a variety of cover-ups. And then, he chose the most risky cover-up of all to hide his heart forever. Drugs.

This made her and his friends and family sad. The drugs did indeed hide his heart. They had always liked his soft heart. They told him that many times, but he never heard them.

One day, no one knows why, he made a very courageous decision. He decided to let his soft heart show. All drugs stopped. All cover-ups gone.

She and his friends and family were happy to see his true heart again. They told him again they had always loved his soft heart... and this time he heard them.

THE PROMISE

My father and I were very close. He was a retired army colonel, with the outward appearance of a rough, tough John Wayne-type guy. In actuality, he was a cream puff with a soft middle. This soft middle was in perpetual search of God. He wasn't looking for a religion. He was looking for God.

He had not been raised in a religion. He felt shortchanged in this, feeling that all children should be raised in a religion, even if they rebelled later. It gave them a bias, a necessary bias, a base-line from which to field their ultimate perceptions of God. He felt that as an adult without a bias, his search for God had a stark objectivity that made it difficult for him to "choose" a religion. They all had many excellent points.

In Dad's search for God he studied the major religions of the world as well as some of the new trendy ones.

I had been raised Catholic by Mom, but as I grew up I began to wear my Catholicism loosely. I joined Dad in reading books and studying various concepts of God. Together, we attended classes and lectures on a multitude of spiritual concepts. Dad and I made a deal that whoever died first would come back and tell the other what it was like.

Dad died in 1981.

Shortly after he died I had what most people would call a dream. It wasn't a dream. It had a strange and beautiful texture, more like that of reality, but clearer, sharper, more real than reality. In the "dream" we were walking down an ordinary street. I knew he was dead. I glibly asked him if other people could see him too, or did I look like a fool, talking to empty space? He calmly said, "It doesn't matter."

I had never seen Dad look so young, but what really struck me was that he looked so content, so peaceful, so deeply happy. We passed by an old fence. There was a loose board, which he moved aside. We stepped through to the other side of the fence and found ourselves in an old junkyard and lumberyard. We sat down on a pile of lumber. He put his arm around me. (At this point in the story, I feel his arms around me, as I did then, and cry.)

He proceeded to tell me "how it all works." I remember that as I listened to him, a feeling swept over me that it all made such beautiful, perfect sense. How could we not have known? How kind it all was. How loving. How perfect the plan.

When I "woke up," I didn't remember the specifics of what he had told me, but I did have the overwhelming knowledge that life was ... more perfect, more fair, more loving, than our tiny brains were capable of imagining.

I live with this wonderful knowing that "now" is beautiful and "later," in another place, is beautiful too. And when we use the term, "a just and loving God," we have no idea how hugely true this is.

And maybe, just maybe, Dad wanted me to tell you this in a book so you too could know.

Thanks, Dad.

WHITE-HOT HATE

I hated her. It was a white-hot hate.

She had once worked for me as my assistant. We had worked together for a year. When she got a better job offer, I was happy for her. The day she left, we exchanged warm good-byes. We hugged each other, promising to stay in touch.

I had a high-profile job with a high-profile company. I got the job while I was going through an all-time low, my divorce. This job had given me back my self-esteem. My co-workers had become my family.

In the seventh year of my employment the company started having financial problems. They needed to let me go. I felt like a queen fallen from grace. My heart was broken. I loved my family but had to leave. When the news leaked out, my co-workers tiptoed around me. No one knew what to say. I felt invisible.

They needed to hire someone cheaper. They did. They hired my ex-assistant. We worked together for three weeks, to make a smooth transition. I had always liked her. I thought she had liked me, too. I was wrong. In the company of others she was charming, caring, and sweet. When we were alone she made snippy remarks and sneered at me with contempt, evidently happy to see the queen fallen. No one else saw. Her dislike of me, her contempt, was obvious, but only to me. I felt even more alone.

I remember vividly one particular moment in the elevator. Just she and I. She spoke to me icily. I don't remember what she said, but I do remember feeling the thickness of her disdain. I knew, at that moment, I was not imagining nonexistent enemies. I had never felt such coldness from anyone, ever. It was chilling. I searched for a reason. What had I ever done to her?

I recalled a Fourth of July family picnic. Her family picnic. She had casually mentioned the planned festivities, a big Italian family gathering. It sounded like fun. I asked her if my son and I could join her and her family. I was longing for a big family get-together, even if not my own. We were so small a family, just the two of us, my young son and me. I wanted us to be a bigger family or at least a part of someone else's bigger family. She hesitated slightly before she said yes. I considered later that perhaps I had put her in an uncomfortable position. I was her boss. Of course, she had to say yes.

At the picnic she was distant and cold. I thought it was just my imagination, with only a fleeting thought that perhaps I had done something wrong in asking to be a part of her day. I never considered that we might be intruders. I chose to ignore the gust of icy coldness I felt that day, the same chill that was to blow through me later, at my most vulnerable time.

Still, I had thought she liked me then. Or maybe she did—some. Or maybe all along she had wanted to be the queen.

She was very smart. I think she knew that. She was also strong. I don't think she knew that. Upon her return, she wielded her newfound power viciously over someone who no longer had power. She kicked me when I was already down, and this she did skillfully, with precision. It was unforgivable. It was the ultimate cruelty. She hurt me badly at a time I was already hurt. She made me feel small when I was already small. She made me feel so alone. And I hated her for that.

This feeling of hate was new to me. I had never been able to stay mad at people, even when I wanted to. My container for anger is built like a strainer. It just sifts out. But this was different. Even after I left the company and no longer saw her I still felt the hate. My strainer had clogged up. I couldn't get rid of this. I meditated and prayed for its release. It felt like an unnatural, foreign substance intruding on my heart. There was a big rip running through me, tearing at me. It hurt to have it. I wanted it off.

Time went by, time spent trying to get the sticky hate off me, without success. I spoke to my friend, Lillian, about it. Lillian is so cool. She told me to enjoy it. Roll around in it, like a pig in mud. I decided to try.

I began to relax with the hate. To accept it. To roll around in it as Lillian suggested. No guilt. Just a feeling. As true, as pure, as valid as any of the other "sweet" feelings I'd happily accepted all my life. The hate left.

I am no longer afraid of any feeling. As for the feelings I don't

19

like, I simply roll around with them playfully like a pig in mud.
And they go away.

The Womb

When my son was in the womb, he was easier to care for. No
sassing. No temper tantrums. I didn't hear the constant, defiant
NO!

I used to threaten him that if he didn't behave he was going
back in the womb. One day, I'd had enough and said, "Okay,
that's it! Give me your foot!" He ran from the room. Not surprisingly, he shaped up for quite a long time after that.

Head and Heart

I learned matters of the head from Dad.
I learned matters of the heart from Mom.

What I learned from Dad
allows people
to see
who I am.
Success, money, cool cars, and
the ability to have intellectual discussions.

What I learned from Mom
allows people
to feel
who I am.
My heart.

PINK

Mom always says,
"Just be happy."
I used to think it was
a silly, weightless
thing to say.

Now,
I realize
the magnificence
of this simple truth
she had given me
all along.

MY NAME IS JOAN

You can see her on bright sunny days when the whole world feels
playful. She wanders the streets. The people in town simply call
her "the homeless lady." They don't know her name. They don't
think of asking.

Her hair is matted, tufts of hair shoot out in all directions,
like an exploded star. Her face is weathered and toughened. It
is far beyond "tan." It is the color of driftwood.

When she was born her mother must surely have cooed sweet
baby sounds to her. Family and friends must have come to see
this beautiful baby girl and remarked how pretty she was.

Maybe she has children, somewhere. Maybe she was married,
with a house, a dog, a shiny kitchen floor, and a husband who
came home to her after work. Maybe she had dinner waiting for
him. Surely, she must have felt love, some time ago.

She has fallen through a crack. The crack is too deep to crawl
out of. She can only look up and see people above, walking
around, who did not fall ... in the crack.

Sometimes rich people give her money. As they hand her the

money, they also give her instructions. "Get something hot to eat with this." She hardly ever does. But mostly it's the poor people who give her money. They give her no instructions.

She wears glasses. They're always dirty. Someone must have given them to her. I wonder if they could possibly be the right prescription. Her clothes are tattered. She finds things in the garbage. Sometimes she smells like Jean Naté. Sometimes she doesn't. She has teeth missing. At times, just for a moment, she forgets she's in the crack, and smiles. Between her missing teeth, joy beams out brightly, perhaps reflecting remnants of memories from days gone by. When she sleeps she surely must dream. Maybe wonderful dreams laced with golden moments. Bright moments of the past and perhaps even splendid dreams of a future filled with luck and happiness.

She lives on the streets and back alleys of Los Gatos, California, an affluent town with affluent people. She sees the contrast. She knows full well that she has fallen through a crack. She also knows that even someone in the crack has a name.

Her name is ... Joan.

BLAME

Leslie told me
she can't afford
any more
blame.
She had accumulated
too much.
That pocket was full.

She decided
to go into a
blameless
phase of her life.

PLAY BALL

Leslie also said…
She wants to "play ball,"
but no one
will throw her the ball.

She's decided
to just take the ball
and run with it.

TWO FRIENDS

There were two friends. As one of the friends grew older she
grew more specific. She liked to collect rules for her life and
now had quite a collection. The rules squeezed her life smaller
and smaller. She liked her life small, palm-size so she could hold
it in her hands.

She wore only clothes that were off-white, black, brown, or
a certain shade of blue. She never wore red. She had had her

"colors done." Red was not acceptable. She would meet friends for a "Happy Hour" drink after work only every third Tuesday of the month, or Wednesdays if it wasn't raining, or Friday nights if it wasn't windy, and she would travel no more than four miles to get to where they were meeting.

As the other friend grew older, she grew less specific. Her wardrobe consisted of every color, including chartreuse, a color she knew didn't really look that good on her. She didn't care. She wore colors based on her mood, not on how she looked. She especially liked red. She had never had her "colors done," not wanting to risk losing any of her favorite colors or, actually, any colors at all.

She filled her days with an eclectic potpourri of people, which included ex-junkies, artists, prostitutes, senators, and judges. Her life was full of variety, chaos, and fun.

The specific friend surrounded her life with other specific people who also collected rules. They were all business people. She and her friends always wore business suits for work, and on their days off wore jeans that were ironed and tennis shoes that had no scuffs and looked new. Her life was controllable and dusty and beige.

One day, the friendship could no longer stand the contrast. It died.

Ouija

One evening
Dad and I were playing
with the Ouija board.

I blindfolded him
to prevent cheating.
He asked the question,
"When will I die?"

The pointer moved to
"No"
then to the number "1"
then to "No" again,
then to the number "1" again.

Then it spelled out the word "dies."

"No 1, No 1, dies."

Except for the spelling,
it was an amazing
goose-bumping
moment.

The Pout

Candace knew him when he had been a prominent artist. He
was a good man. He lived in California, in the town of Loma
Prieta. During the Loma Prieta earthquake, he lost everything
he owned on the outside and on the inside. In addition to his
furniture and personal belongings, his paintings had been de-
stroyed. His life turned sour.

Candace watched him as he began to pout. He didn't work
on his art. He wasn't a bad man. He wasn't a good man. He was
and did nothing for eight years.

In the ninth year, having become bored with the pout, and perhaps fearing that he might lose himself forever in the purgatory of pouting, he began to emerge. Candace got him a job where she worked. He became a teacher and a kind of social worker, working with teenagers, some of whom had experienced physical abuse from time to time, but all of whom had been beaten up emotionally on a regular basis.

He taught his students how to color outside the lines in ways that wouldn't get them arrested and would fill in the vacant spaces in their hearts. He showed them how to color their hearts lavender, which is the color of hope and how to think in new ways by teaching them how to take their fear and use it to power their creativity. He taught them how to move a crystal on the end of a chain using just their minds and how to paint wild and beautiful pictures of wild and beautiful things, like themselves. He showed them the reflection of their own power. They loved him. His goodness was back.

Candace talked to him from time to time about getting back into his art. He seemed not to hear her. Then, early one evening while Candace was working late, he called to tell her that he had left some important papers at school. He asked if she would bring them to him on her way home. Of course she would. She knew he lived in the mountains, but had never been to his house. She gathered his papers and carefully followed the directions he had given her.

She wound around curvy mountain roads until she suddenly happened upon an odd glow in the deep forest night. She slowed down, trying to understand the eerie light that made the forest shadows dance. She rounded a bend and her mouth fell agape as she came upon the source of the flickering lights.

He had set up his home in the forest. There was no house, but there was indeed a home. The treetops were his roof, the pine-needled floor his carpet. Tucked into every tree trunk, every crevice in the forest, were hundreds of candles, throwing off dancing lights that licked the scenery with each gentle breeze.

In the center of the clearing, was the "living room." Two overstuffed chairs sat facing each other, with wide, comfortable arms and tall, elegant backs. They were upholstered in blood-red velvet and accented with silk throw pillows the color of gold doubloons. In front of the chairs sat a cocktail table with a wrought-iron base shaped in the form of graceful vines and topped by thick beveled glass. A few leaves had artfully fallen onto the glass.

The "bedroom" had a king-size sleigh bed of highly polished walnut. On top of the bed lay a Ralph Lauren brocade comforter in moss green and gold. A hand-painted French armoire stood next to a giant redwood. Alongside the armoire stood an easel made from birch-tree branches, and resting on the easel was a magnificent painting of his forest home.

As delicate sounds of Vivaldi's *The Four Seasons* came from his stereo, bathing the forest in music, he greeted her, explaining that this was his summer home. He then served her the best martini she'd ever had.

She knew the pouting was over. This beautiful man had found himself once again, and all was right with the world.

I Release You

Our cat's name was Blue. She was twenty-four years old, a generous age for a cat. She had outlasted my marriage. I loved her.

One day Blue became very ill. I knew she was dying. I took her to the vet, who confirmed my diagnosis. There was nothing to do but make her as comfortable as possible and ... wait. Days went by. The old girl hung on, refusing to die.

One night as I was petting Blue, I remembered a story from the book *Autobiography of a Yogi,* the story of Paramhansa Yogananda's life. When Paramhansa was a young boy, he found a fawn whose mother had died. Paramhansa took care of the deer, which grew up and became his constant companion and best friend.

Some years later the deer became very ill and, like Blue, refused to die. The deer clung to life with a sad, stubborn determination. One night, the deer came to Paramhansa in a dream. He told the boy he was ready to die, ready for his new adventure, but the boy's love was keeping him earthbound. The deer told Paramhansa he loved him, but it was time for him to go. He asked Paramhansa to release him. The boy awoke, and with tearful eyes held his friend as he said, "I release you." That night, the deer died.

With the memory of Paramhansa's story prompting me, I held Blue and told her that I released her, sending her off to her next joyful adventure. Days went by; her condition worsened, and still she would not, did not, die.

Thinking that maybe I wasn't the only one who had to release Blue, I told my eight-year-old son, Toby, the story of Paramhansa and the deer. Toby held Blue gently as he said, "I release you." That night, Blue died.

Time passed and our tears dried. One day, Toby's grandmother, "Abuelita," came by, and she and Toby got into a heated argument. Toby looked her straight in the eye and said, "I release you."

I looked at Toby with astonishment. With a twinkle in his eye he said, "Just kidding." Abuelita, of course, had no idea of what had just occurred. Somehow, in his eight years of not-so-wise wisdom, he felt he now had the power of life and death.

Today, Toby is twenty-three years old, and I'm glad to report that he has never "released" anybody again. And we think of Blue often and with love.

SCREAMING IN THE GROCERY STORE

Before I had a child, I would see a woman in the grocery store whose child was screaming in an uncontrollable temper tantrum, and think, "Why doesn't she control her child?!" Then, I had a child.

I would go to the grocery store and my sweet angel would throw a fit punctuated by a series of bloodcurdling screams. Invariably, I would see a woman who had not yet had children and who mistakenly thought the little beasts were controllable, as I had once thought. She looks at me with the same look I used to give. A look that says, "Why don't you control your child?!"

I walk away, looking back at her with resigned indignity and shrug my shoulders helplessly.

Moral: If we live long enough, life will turn around and bite us in the ass.

The Christmas Letter, 1995

(Excerpts printed in *Chicken Soup for the Soul:
A Christmas Treasury.*)

When I get mass-mailed letters from friends at Christmas, it makes me feel like my life is all wrong. The lives they portray are so perfect: well-behaved children winning awards, husbands getting job promotions, the family buying beautiful new homes overlooking golf courses, and vacationing in exotic lands.

One year, I decided to send a "gift" in the form of a Christmas letter to all my friends, to tell honestly how my life was going and to make them feel wonderful about theirs.

Here's the letter:

Dear Family and Friends,

Well, the Christmas season has arrived and once again I find myself:

___ With all my Christmas shopping done, the tree up, and money left over.

_X_ A day late and lots of dollars short.

Carmen:

Carmen has quit smoking

___ Yeah, right.

_X_ Has actually quit, but has also been chewing Nicorette gum for three years and finds that she can, in essence, "smoke" in theaters, restaurants, the shower, and the most fun of all, health food stores. She is planning on looking into a methadone program to help her get off the gum.

___ Who's Carmen?

Carmen's advertising agency:
____ Has flourished, and now she has a staff of twenty and wears indecently expensive designer suits.

____ Went belly up. Carmen is now homeless and enjoying the freedom.

____ Was unaffected by the recession.

_X_ Had some rough "recessive" times, but the year turned out to be fairly decent. (In all fairness, however, one might be prompted to ask for clarification of the term "fairly decent," considering two refinances of her house in a one-year period.)

Carmen has a boyfriend.
____ A boyfriend—yeah, right.

_X_ Yes, she does! His name is Glen and he's a pretty regular guy, except he thinks he's from the planet Ektar.

The boyfriend's family:
____ Is not just as loony as Carmen's family.

_X_ Do not think Glen is from Ektar.

Carmen's hair color:
_X_ Got red all by itself, quite naturally. Simultaneously, the gray magically disappeared, and no one knows why her eyebrows and "hidden hairs" are still brown.

____ Who cares?

Carmen is growing older:
____ With style and grace.

____ Style and grace—yeah, right.

____ Refuses to.

_X_ Miraculously, got stuck in a time warp at the age of twenty-five and has not aged since.

Carmen is:

____ Looking great "for her age." (I hate that expression.)

____ "Help, my eyelids are falling and they can't get up."

____ Wears lip liner to prevent her lipstick from creeping up the lip crevices onto other parts of her face.

_X_ How's the weather been?

Carmen's weight gain:

____ "Skinny Carmen" gaining weight? Never.

____ Has filled out nicely.

____ Is fat

_X_ Boy, that weather!

My Son Toby

Toby is:

____ On the honor roll.

_X_ Got an "A" in wrestling.

____ Who's Toby?

Toby went to his first semiformal Coronation Ball, rented a forty-foot limousine with his buddies, had a very cute date, wore a tuxedo, and looked:

____ Very ugly.

____ Like a pimply-faced grownup.

_X_ Oh-so-handsome!

THE REST OF THE FAMILY:

MOM

____ Finally turned into a normal mom just like June Cleaver and now bakes.

____ Fell in love with a Spanish count and is living in a castle in Southern Spain.

_X_ Is, I'm convinced, from another planet, but we love her nonetheless (and I'm sure I'm adopted).

DAD

____ Started exercising, lost weight, and is studying classical piano.

____ Faked his death and is now living happily in Brazil with a cute little native chick.

_X_ Did die, but lives in all our hearts and wants to be included in this Christmas newsletter. (We love you, Dad.)

MY BIG BROTHER JOHNNY

_X_ Is from the same planet Mom's from.

____ Has a daughter, Jill, who's *not* the apple of his eye.

_X_ Has a lovely wife, Marilyn, who's about as normal as Johnny.

And

_X_ Has gone "ethnic" and calls himself "Juan."

____ Doesn't still dress like a hippie, or wear the same leather belt he wore in the '70s.

____ Is an average kind of fellow.

_X_ Is, was, and always will be ... just weird.

MY LITTLE SISTER PIXIE

_X_ Is growing more "normal" every day, to the extent that Mom is "normal."

____ Owns a residential construction company along with hubby, David, and their business has been untouched by the recession.

And

____ Has two children, Tyler and Dominee, who never disobey, don't sass back, and who's only desires are to please their parents.

_X_ Is still trying to play grownup and now calls herself "Maria."

____ Is looking younger every day.

____ Who's Pixie? She sounds like a stripper.

THE ANIMALS:

RUFUS, THE BASSET HOUND

_X_ If you touch him, your hand stinks.

_X_ Pees in the house.

____ Is very obedient and can run with lighting speed.

BLUE, THE TWENTY-YEAR-OLD CAT (PEOPLE YEARS)

____ Is still quite spry and has not turned cranky in her old age.

 X Looks like a skinny cat version of a bag lady.

BABY, THE COCKATOO

____ Carmen had a baby?

 X Bites Carmen all the time.

 X Has successfully chewed up most of her room, and yes, she does have her own room.

THE GUINEA PIGS

____ Have been trained to ride itty-bitty bicycles.

 X Just stay in their cage and stink up Toby's room. (They *do not* have their own room.)

CHRISTMAS

Christmas is:

____ Time to put on your bathing suit and go to the beach.

____ Time to put out American flags and light firecrackers.

 X Time to sing "Happy Birthday" to someone in the form of Christmas carols.

Finally, The End:

Carmen and her family

____ Are living a life of style, grace, and harmony that resembles a Norman Rockwell painting.

_X_ Are all doing fine, which means we're taking life as it comes, with its great variety of surprises, disappointments, and delights, and always, always, find it interesting and a joy to be a part of.

MERRY CHRISTMAS TO YOU ALL!

"Eat, drink, enjoy the Earth,
and feed your love for all it's worth."

LOVE,
Carmen
Toby
&
All the little creatures of the house.

Chapter 2

MODERN DANCE ~
TODAY'S WORLD

Modern dance gyrates with the movements of today's world. This dance is fast, hectic, and ever changing. The steps are temporarily in vogue, with tomorrow's steps waiting just around the corner to replace today's. Popular old dance steps fall by the way. We twirl and spin and sometimes get dizzy. Still, we keep on dancing, waiting for instructions on tomorrow's exciting new steps.

THE EXTRA HALF-HOUR

I found half an hour lying on the ground. I bent down, picked it up, and put it in my pocket. I wasn't sure what to do with it. I thought about spending it on feeling lonely or sad. I considered spending it thinking of all the productive things I could be doing with it, and spend the half-hour on feeling guilty. Instead, I decided to just sit outside with it.

The sun began to fall, and sparrows made twittering bird noises, arguing back and forth as they vied for position on the branches of the giant oak. This was their neighborhood. They were settling in for the evening. A single mockingbird made laughing sounds at the silly sparrows. Mockingbirds need no special branch on which to sleep. Statuesque pines bent in the wind, their tips pointing, a ballerina's arms.

My parrot, Baby, sat on my shoulder, cracking sunflower seeds. When she was full, she tucked one leg up into her feathers and fanned out her cheek feathers alongside her beak. She was content, happy that I had invited her along on this extra half-hour I'd found.

Two bicyclists sped by us on the street. Their portable CD players blasted music, intruding on nature's serene sounds. Occasionally, a car passed by with people going from Point A to Point B. As they sped by, I wondered if they noticed me, not having to rush anywhere, with my extra half-hour.

Nature's shapes were thrown on the grass in long dark shadows. The shapes changed gracefully as the sun fell. The shadows moved so slowly with the sun's descent that I could see what had changed, but could not see the changing.

I thought of my life, and how I could also see what had changed, but could not see the changing. I would awaken to a day, dark and stormy or bright with sun, but always different, always interesting. Always the day, new. And sometimes this new day would bring an extra half-hour lying on the ground.

WHITE

Who thought
of calling clear wine
"white"?
And what color
does that make
milk?

COLORS

Male energy is, of course,
deep blue.
Female energy, however,
is, surprisingly, not pink,
but purple —
a combination of deep blue and pink.

Contrary to popular thought,
women in today's world
are not trying to be blue,
but purple.

It is true that once in a while
we stumble across a woman or two
who are trying to be blue,
and this confuses men.
But, really, most of us
just want to
be the lovely purple
that we are.

How We See

(Published in *Chicken Soup for the Unsinkable Soul*)

Has anyone ever said,
"It's important
to spend less time
on how we look
and more time
on how we see"?

If not,
perhaps someone should.

The Wrong Class

I drove for an hour and a half to a class on "How to get your book published." When I arrived I discovered I had come on the wrong day.

I was naturally upset at my stupidity as I walked to the "Women's Room." When I arrived at my destination I stopped and stared at the door. The "W" had fallen off "Women" leaving "omen." I was sure it was.

I checked the classes scheduled for that night, looking for one that was sure to be my destiny. There was a class on how to quit smoking. No, I had my Nicorette. There was another class on how to live without stress. No, stress and I have, at long last, become friends. Finally, I saw a class that held promise. It was a class on quantum physics and the soul. Yes ... maybe.

I decided to take the class. I ended up sitting through three long, boring hours, listening to how new scientific theories are being used in an attempt to try to prove the existence of God. What I discovered was, I don't need science to prove the existence of God, any more than I need God to prove the existence of science.

What have I learned? I've learned that sometimes when the "W" is missing from the Women's Room door, it's simply the "W" missing from the Women's Room door.

To Don't List

Don't ever suppress a laugh
~ it causes heart disease.
Don't spit upwind
~ you know why.
Don't ever disbelieve a compliment
~ fight your instincts and believe it.
Don't ever disbelieve someone who says, "I love you"
~ it's too hard to come by, and it might be true.
Don't ever tell someone, "You don't love me"
~ they might believe you.
Don't ever be in love … alone.
Don't be too sad, too long
~ you can get stuck there.
Don't suppress happiness
~ even if you look stupid.
Don't ever call yourself stupid
~ people might believe you.
Don't ever use the word "but" in an apology.
Don't give an honest answer
~ if a friend asks if you like her ugly dress.
Don't use the words "should" or "shouldn't,"
~ in a sentence with the words, "feel," "think," or "be."
Don't clean your no-wax floor with Comet.
~The same is true for your plastic-lens glasses.
Don't stop looking at your reflection in store windows.
Don't cross your eyes in a big wind
~ Mom says they'll stay that way.
Don't pick your nose while in a car

~ people can *see* you.

Don't sue anyone lightly

~ life is random and not all misfortunes are blamable. (It's why we have the word "accident" in the dictionary.)

Don't finish reading a book if you've decided you don't like it.

Don't finish a piece of chocolate candy that you don't like

~ take a bite and put the rest back in the box.

Don't think in small numbers.

Don't cross out anything you've done

~ anyway, you can't.

Don't put fingernail polish on your lips

~ it doesn't work as all-day lipstick, and it hurts.

Don't try to spell *hors d'oeuvres* without a dictionary.

Don't tell someone you don't love them

~ say something else.

Don't visit denial too long.

Don't listen to someone who says, "Have a good life"

~ it's sarcasm.

FLOW

Someone once told me
to get in the flow.

Oh, my God—
There's a flow?!

LUNCH AT CAFE MARCELLA

The couple was a middle-aged version of nerds. He was skinny and wore a tight, probably inexpensive, dark blue sweater. The sweater had been in fashion ten years ago. He was balding, and the few hairs that remained shot out in a multitude of directions. Atop his nose rested metal-framed eyeglasses with thick lenses that made his eyes look abnormally large.

She too wore glasses, with thin, faded, plastic frames that were, I'm sure, originally brown—plain brown, not tortoise. She wore a blue suit, a blue that almost had its own name, but not quite. It was not light blue, dark blue, sky blue, baby blue, or navy blue. It was nondescript blue. It was *almost* blue, lacking the courage to be an actual blue. The suit had straight lines. It was plain. She wore a cotton blouse that had little flowers with a hint of the almost blue in their tiny petals. Dangling drop earrings of black onyx hung beneath her ears, and swung wildly in pendulum fashion when she moved her head even slightly. Her hair was cut in a bob, parted down the middle, with bangs resting on the top of her eyeglasses. Her limp, baby-fine hair was a limp brown color.

I guessed her to be a librarian or some sort of scientist. He, I'm sure, was an engineer, or also some sort of scientist. The conversation between the couple never had an awkward moment or pregnant pause. It rolled along interestingly. It had momentum and fun to it. They liked talking to each other. They liked each other. Their energy together was lively.

When their champagne arrived, he checked the bottle and gave his approval as she talked and laughed with the French waiter. She laughed loudly, and as she did, the other patrons looked at her as if she'd broken a secret rule. She did not notice their disapproving glances. She began to speak French to the waiter. Her French sported a flat American accent. The waiter looked pleased that she was attempting her version of French with him. Her partner gave a big, wide smile, proud of her ability with languages.

In this fancy, casually elegant, upscale restaurant, the patrons were equally fancy, casually elegant, and upscale. They were intrinsically aware of the latest fashion in conversation, gestures, attire, and all the accompanying social graces of the day. Their understanding of fashionable trends was apparent in their clothing, their behavior, the tilt of their heads, and manner of speech. Most of them had a bored, flat look on their faces, which was only occasionally broken by a thin, ungenerous smile. When they wanted to express pleasure they made quiet sounds in the back of their throats, like laughter that had been swallowed. They did not laugh out loud.

As I looked at the couple, in contrast to the other patrons, I felt a warmth deep inside, coupled with a profound respect for them. Unlike the others, they had outgrown their need to impress their classmates. They no longer cared if they were passed over for the cheerleading squad or hadn't made the football team. The others, however, were still caught in the web of wanting to be chosen for the team. They were still striving to be popular, part of the in-crowd. Perhaps they did not realize the price they were paying for their petrified dreams. The cost of stifled laughter ... for dreams that should have been left in high school.

GOSSIP

People know their lives are full
when they don't have time for
small, petty gossip.

Big, juicy gossip,
however,
there's always time for.

SUNGLASSES

I bought a pair of sunglasses. They were very stylish. I looked cool.

There was, however, one problem, the lenses were tinted brown. They made the sky look brown, the trees brown, and the brown smog browner. I wanted a happy-colored lens, like blue, to make the blue sky bluer, the trees a deep bluish green, and the smog blue, like the sky should be. I found myself pondering the question, "What's more important, the way the I see the world, or the way the world sees me?"

I kept the sunglasses and had the lenses tinted blue. And so, the question goes unanswered, at least, for the moment.

Toys

He who dies
with the most toys
gets to watch
as other people
play with them.

Pennies

I met a man who picked up pennies
he found on the ground.
"Because," he said,
"they're government property."

I pick up pennies
because I see them as signs
from angels, letting us know
they're around,
kind of like
angel droppings.

VOGUE PARTIES

I always had the feeling
there were parties
I never knew about,
where all the woman
wore clothes
from *Vogue* magazine.

I never saw these
strange and beautiful clothes
on anyone, ever.
There had to be
secret, fancy parties
that people like me
were not invited to,
where women were dressed
in *Vogue* fashions.

One day, while glancing through *Vogue*
there, to my astonishment,
was a blouse
just like the one
I had bought the week before,
on sale.

I realized at that moment
that there were no secret, fancy parties.
Or, if there were,
I was already
at the party.

CODEPENDENCY

It's a good thing
Mother Teresa
never heard the terms
"codependent"
or "enabling."

SOME DAYS

Why is it that some days everyone seems to want me, wants to be around me, wants to be part of my life. Other days, I could strip naked and run down the street, and no one would give me the slightest glance?

To me, I look basically the same on both days. Do I have a beautiful aura that's partially visible some days and entirely invisible other days? Or maybe, on my visible days, I emit a wonderful scent that only others can smell, and it attracts them to me, kind of like a whistle audible only to dogs. If I could capture the knowledge of the difference from day to day, I could be ever visible, ever desirable, every day and forever.

Great men have said that one cannot know joy without knowing sorrow, cannot know peace without war, cannot know happiness without pain. So, I ask myself, would my visible days be as much fun if I were visible every day and forever?

Yes. Absolutely. I continue the search.

Road Signs

Whenever she had a big decision to make, she'd pay attention to road signs.

YIELD would sometimes jump right out at her, and she knew she had to back off and let others pass. Other times, MERGE would appear before her, and she knew she had to compromise. STOP was a message that was quite clear, "Don't do it." Yellow lights, especially in succession, meant "Proceed with caution." A series of green lights meant "Full speed ahead." Although CHILDREN AT PLAY was a bit nebulous, it mostly meant people were just playing with her emotions.

Even though her major decisions were based on what her friends considered foolish notions, her life went along quite well. And when she made mistakes, she figured she just hadn't read the signs right.

Morning Pages

Morning pages. Writing practice for my book. It's a rainy Sunday morning. My 50 percent silk pajamas feel good against my skin. They feel like 100 percent silk. The Christmas tree has been bought, lugged into the house and stands waiting for its holiday jewelry.

The house is still, except for the delicate sounds of classical music that fill the living room, making the house look cleaner than it is and making my life feel more gracious than it is. At this precise moment, I feel pampered.

Accompanied by a cup of cappuccino, I sit on the sofa with pen poised and paper before me, ready to write what might be great literary works — or at least decent writing. As I begin to write, the page starts to show promise, strings of words begin to germinate from seedlings of thought.

Suddenly, Romulus, our puppy, leaps onto my lap. His muddy

paw stamps the page with a brown paw print. He chews the edge of the paper and then pushes my pen with his nose. My neat writing becomes jagged scribbles as I rush to finish putting this "one last thought" on paper before it's lost forever. Romulus then begins to lick my face, a last attempt to make his unwilling partner play with him. He wins. I stop and hug him.

Once he's got my attention, Romulus gets bored and leaves. I attempt to get back to my writing. The doorbell rings. My son's friends are looking for the CD they left in his car. The phone rings: Mom wants to know what she should get my sister for Christmas. Baby, the cockatoo, starts to scream, demanding sunflower seeds. Romulus lifts his leg on the Christmas tree ... and pees. Toby wakes up and wants to know where the bacon is, where the eggs are, where the bread is. I get up and make him breakfast.

Finally, Toby leaves and the animals are quiet. I sit down again to write, and find that all my great writing ideas have vanished. As I look at the scene before me, with breakfast dishes piled high, I wonder how great men did great things in the face of real life. I guess they didn't need to tend to the home, the children, the animals. Perhaps they had fewer distracting details to contend with. Perhaps they were born with a single, direct focus and less of a need to deal with life in the peripheral.

Given the choice, which, of course, I don't have, I guess I would choose this life, this life in the peripheral, for there lie the minuscule details of real life that inspire my writing. The chaotic assortment of adventures and misadventures strewn throughout my life give it color, depth, and perspective. Perhaps they offer warmth to what otherwise would indeed be a single, direct focus, but it would be cold. The edges would be hard. The writing would miss the rich little pieces of story that lie hidden in the peripheral.

And so, I put my creativity in the crevices, the in-between times, the times when family, friends, and animals are still. And in those quiet times, I will take pieces of the chaos and commotion and build a mosaic of warmth, passion, and love that can come only from the wide peripheral vision of an ordinary woman who lives in the details of an ordinary life.

WORN SPOT IN THE SKY

There was a worn spot in the sky.
The Earth had exhaled too many times
in the same spot.

The worn spot
allowed too much sun
to touch the Earth.

The people under the spot
became too tan.
Their too-tanned skin
made them look
like they were covered in
a brown paper bag.

In contrast
with their too-brown skin,
their teeth looked
way too white,
iridescent, actually.
God took notice of these people,
and thought their too-white teeth
were scary looking.

He sent a big cloud
to patch up the hole
in the sky,
a Band-Aid
for the sky's wound.

The people lost their tans,
their teeth looked normal
once again,
and all was
good with the world.

God does indeed
watch over us,
and He wants us…
to look good.

New Year's Resolutions, 1998

I will dream louder.
I will show anger softer.
I will try to better recognize and acknowledge the beauty and
wonder that is in everyone.
I will try to better recognize and acknowledge the beauty and
wonder that is in me.
I will be more aware of my power, so I can wield it on purpose
and with a good heart.
I will indulge in benevolence of forethought.
I will laugh as loudly as I want, wherever I want, especially
in libraries and museums.
I will stay centered in myself while loving other people.
I will find a comfortable and easy way to lose weight.
I will find a comfortable and easy way to get out of debt.
I will make money, lots of it, doing something I love.
I will respect and honor other people's differences.
I will respect and honor my differences.
I will work as hard on my dreams as I do on my work.
I will widen my view, shorten my anger, and lengthen
my eyelashes.

I will be a better...
  mother
  daughter
  sister
  friend
  lover
  human being
  Carmen.
I will spread magic whenever possible.
I will love whenever possible.
I will cut down, and possibly quit, Nicorette gum.
I will stop buying so many shampoos, looking for the perfect
hair care product.

Too Pretty

If a flower
looks too pretty,
we say it looks fake.

What a weird thing to say.

Be There

If people tell you
"You're a dreamer,"
"You're not in touch with reality,"
"You're too optimistically 'pink,'"

Tell them
to go away.

The world needs you now.
Be there.

BUSINESS CALL

When you make a business call
And the secretary says,
"Will he know what this is regarding?"
Just tell her,
"Not unless he's clairvoyant."

MAKING A LIVING

I'm
so, so, so, so, so, so, so, so, so, so, so, so, so, so, so, so, so, so, so,
so, so, so, so, so, so, so, so, so, so, so, so, so, so, so, so, so,
so, so, so, so, so, so, so, so, so, so, so, so, so, so, so, so, so, so, so,
so, so, so, so, so, so, so, so, so, so, so, so, so, so, so, so, so,
so, so, so, so, so, so, so, so, so, so, so, so, so, so, so, so, so,
so, so, so, so, so, so, so, so, so, so, so, so, so, so, so, so, so,
so, so, so, so, so, so, so, so, so, so, so, so, so, so, so, so, so,
tired of having to make
a living.

I want life to be...
....
....
....
free.

BAD SHOE SEASON

There are times in life
that are like a bad shoe season.
You just have to let them pass.
And hope for better styles
next season.

THE MASSES

To choose
what the masses
like, want, think,
as your standard,
is choosing
mediocrity.

Choose higher.

IF SOMEONE

If someone screams,
"That's not true!"
it probably is.

If someone screams,
"I don't care!"
they probably do.

If someone screams,
"I love you,"
he probably does.

If someone whispers
gossip,
it's probably not true.

If someone tells gossip
in a strong, true voice
on a bright sunny day,
it's probably true.

If someone whispers,
"I love you,"
in the middle of the day,

without prompting,
it's probably true.

If someone is naked and lying down,
and says, "I love you,"
it could be true or not.
If they're sitting up and naked,
it's probably true.
Anything said while naked
about any subject other than love
is usually true.

If someone says something
while crying,
it's probably true,
but if it's a woman,
it might not be true.
Some women have learned
to cry-lie.

If somebody believes
his or her own lie,
you'll never be able to tell
it's a lie.

If someone never blinks
while talking...
I have no idea.

WHICH HALF?

Mr. Marriott, of the Marriott Corporation
was quoted as saying,
"I know that half
of my advertising
works

and the other half
doesn't.
I just don't know which half
isn't working."

I have a similar feeling
about my life.
Half of my life
is under my control.
The other half is random.
I just don't know
which half
isn't under my control.

So, I try to control everything,
which, of course, only works
fifty percent of the time.

WRITING A NEW BOOK

I'm thinking of writing a book called
Understanding Men.

It would be about 200 pages long.

All the pages would, of course,
be blank.

CRITICISM

I'm not big on criticism. Here's why:

People tell you they're giving you "constructive" criticism.
What is that, and by whose definition is it constructive? I find
that most criticism is de-structive—not all, but definitely most.
Con-structive and de-structive criticisms have different styles

of presentation and they feel differently when you receive them.

If presented skillfully, constructive criticism feels okay when you receive it. It's information you can use to better yourself, something you can construct with. It can even make you feel somehow expanded. Constructive criticism takes real talent to deliver, a talent I don't have, and most people I've met don't have, either.

Destructive criticism is easy to recognize. It doesn't feel good. It destroys. You feel diminished. It makes you feel small.

The validity of criticism depends greatly on who's giving it. Is their opinion worth listening to? Do you respect, love, or admire them to the extent that you trust their ability to make a judgment about you? You will answer yes to some and no to others. I say no to most, but when I say yes, I take their opinions to heart.

How criticism is offered is of supreme importance. If it's offered with intelligence and from the giver's heart, it will feel smooth. It won't sting. If it's given with intelligence but no heart, don't listen. These are just intelligent, but mean, people. If it's given from the heart, but without intelligence, be nice, but again, don't listen, there's no validity. Also, pay more attention to criticism that is "offered," rather than that which is "given." There is a subtle but important difference. Criticism that's "given" feels like it's being crammed down your throat. If it is "offered," it feels like it's presented on a silver platter for you to take or not.

Constructive criticism should consist only of information about ourselves that we aren't already aware of. This is a hard one, as most of us have already beaten ourselves up over every conceivable fault, many times over. We tend to embrace a pattern of masochistic introspection that makes us painfully aware of a multitude of flaws, some of which we actually have, and others I'm sure we don't.

If people want to offer me criticism, I try to let them know that they should couch it in euphemisms, using the sweetest words at their disposal, so that it's just barely recognizable as criticism. Most of us are hypersensitive to criticism, and a little bit goes a long way. Additionally, constructive criticism must be about something that is correctable. Criticizing someone about something they can't change is just mean. And it should be presented in a non-hurtful way. Like most of us, I reject that which hurts me; I simply close up. If it's said too harshly, I won't listen, and the person giving the criticism will have accomplished nothing, except having made me feel bad about myself—and probably about them.

In the end, I'm not so sure that criticism of either sort is really of much value, as there are far too many criteria for offering the optimal constructive criticism. Most of us just aren't skillful enough to do it well. Besides, great thinkers have said that we tend to get more of what we focus on. Consequently, if we focus on the negative aspects of ourselves rather than on our strengths, we diminish the great gifts of who we *are* by devoting an inordinate amount of time and energy to who we are *not*.

It has also been said that if we focus on our strengths, our weaknesses fall away. So, my suggestion would be to focus on the people who support you and let the others fall away.

A Piece of the Day No One Wants

Vivaldi's home in Venice. A wonderful accident to be staying here, a mix-up with the hotel reservation, a serendipitous mix-up. Our suite was once Vivaldi's bedroom. It is filled with dark, massive antiques, and has a window on one side of the room that overlooks one of Venice's minor canals.

Outside the window, across the canal live two old women. I've watched them for three days. They appear to be sisters. I somehow imagine them to be spinsters. They're always dressed in black from head to toe, with black lace that comes to a point between their middle and index fingers. They seem to be from another century. I see them taking turns during the day, feeding the pigeons that land on their sill. I never see them speak to each other. They are never together, except for passing in the hallway. Perhaps they're encrusted in an old family spat that has gone on for many years, but through necessity are forced to live together. Perhaps it's an argument they don't even remember, but continue the pattern that has gone on for so long and that they're now so comfortable with.

On the other side of Vivaldi's room, the window overlooks a serene garden, ripe with antiquity and surrounded by a moss-covered stone wall that hides the secret garden from the scurrying crowds of Venice, just on the other side. Playful sparrows flit about the garden, with no knowledge of the great priest who composed light, airy music, so much like their little songs.

I go down to the garden and sit in the waning afternoon sun. This is a useless time of day that no one wants—it's the day's intermission. People are busily ending afternoon events or preparing for evening occasions to come. This is a transitional time of day that no one claims. As I sit in Vivaldi's garden, writing in my journal, I sip red wine and munch on salty snacks, listening to the music of the flighty birds, and claim as mine this piece of the day no one wants.

GEAR REVERSAL

I scream
upwind.

It blows back
into my mouth.
No one hears.
I am left
to swallow it.

I am
an uninvited guest
at the party.
I am overdressed.
I am too shiny.
I do not fit in.

At parties
where everyone
is wearing black,
I end up wearing white.
The parties
where everyone
is wearing white,
I wear black.
I never get it right.

I am
a swollen pimple
on life's glorious,
perfect plan.

I write too many words
for a poem,
too few
for a story.

Gr-r-r-r-r-i-n-d
The sound of gears reversing.

Actually,
to scream upwind
and catch it
in one's own mouth,
is a phenomenal feat.
Screams
actually have a flavor.
They taste good.

As for being
an uninvited guest,
if I'm here,
I must
have been invited.

As far as
being too shiny,
well, can anyone
ever really be
too shiny?

To wear black
at the white-wearing parties
and white
at the black-wearing parties,
gives a nice accent
to what might otherwise be
a monochromatic event.

And I think
that maybe
I'm not a pimple,
but rather

an interesting birthmark,
to remind us
how really boring
perfection
can be.

Too many words,
too few words,
to fit a literary format,
I'll make up a new
literary format.

Fall - Daytime

It is fall and I wake up sleepy. The trees and flowers remain asleep as I begin my day and walk though the sleepy web that the autumn weaves. I must get up and go to work. I must be involved in the day. I must participate. The plants and trees grow slowly inward and downward, saving their life energy for spring. For now, they sleep. As a human, I am subject to human rules and codes of human behavior and have to work with the same fervor in fall's sleepy time as in spring's awake time. It is contrary to nature. I want to crawl into a damp, dark cave and hibernate with the bears. I want to huddle up against their warmth, using their teddy-bear fur as my pillow. But no, it's off to work I go. I'm so-o-o-o sleepy.

Fall - Nighttime

The fall evening contains the sounds of an empty can. Hollow, wailing sounds echo against tin sides. Trees yawn as they begin their long sleep. Green buds release breathy sighs and are pushed root-ward. Pastels change to tones of brown. Tulip bulbs sleep beneath the frost-covered dirt, hoping for one more spring. Crisp air turns sharply cold. Human breath fogs the air. The bright harvest moon displays itself in sharp edges against the black night. I long for summer's moon with its soft, airbrushed edges that blend with the evening. But it is fall. The moon is sharp and cold. It is late and I cannot sleep.

IF THEY ASK

At the drugstore, I was standing in line behind a customer who was giving the sales clerk a hard time. The dowdy, middle-aged woman was trying to buy ten pair of pantyhose at the previous week's sale price.

The sales clerk politely told her that the sale was last week and the sale price was no longer valid. The woman said she couldn't come to the store last week, as she'd been sick with the flu and couldn't leave the house. She insisted on being charged the sale price for the pantyhose. The salesgirl apologetically told the woman she could not sell her the items at the discounted price. It was against store policy, and she would get in trouble. Her register wouldn't even ring them up at the sale price.

The woman demanded to see the manager, but the manager was not available, as he was on his dinner break and had left the store. The woman began to yell and curse at the little sales clerk, whose face was getting red as she grew more and more flustered. This went back and forth for a few minutes, the woman's voice growing louder and louder. The clerk began to cry.

As I stood, watching the scene unfold, the woman suddenly turned to me and said, "What are you looking at?!" Without hesitation, I replied, "An idiot." She huffed and snorted and left the store. The salesgirl thanked me.

I have since decided that whenever someone asks me that rhetorical question, I will indeed answer.

I DON'T TRUST PEOPLE WHO —

~ don't like dogs
~ aren't liked by dogs
~ don't have any friends
~ have too many friends
~ never complain
~ always complain
~ are never crabby
~ never admit they're crabby when they are
~ like dogs, but not cats
~ like cats, but not dogs
~ never get mad
~ say they're "angry" instead of "mad"
~ are too white
~ never disagree with me
~ always disagree with me
~ always use the word "never"
~ always use the word "always"
~ call kids "children"
~ don't love
~ don't hate (except for nuns)
~ are stingy with the word "love"
~ have never been jealous or envious of another person, including their friends
~ don't talk in a silly, high-pitched voice to animals and babies
~ are always "appropriate"
~ use the word "appropriate"
~ snicker, but don't laugh
~ don't ever fight
~ call a fight, a "disagreement"
~ have never at least *wanted* to do something great

And —
~ teenagers who don't fight with their parents
~ people who are on drugs
~ me on drugs
~ men who don't like women
~ women who don't like men
~ people whose parents are their best friends
~ people in love
~ me in love
~ teachers who call their students "people." "People, please be seated."
~ women who don't like sex
~ men who aren't obsessed with sex
~ women who pee on toilet seats in public restrooms
But mostly, I don't trust people who don't trust people.

Staying at The Ritz

I'm here at The Ritz Carlton-Huntington in Pasadena, California, on a business trip. The accommodations were chosen and paid for by a large print company that I contracted to print a catalog for one of my clients. They flew me here for the press check. I'm being wined and dined. It's luscious.

I sit in "The Bar," waiting for the next press check. The bar is so upscale, so cool, it is simply called "The Bar." No further explanation is needed.

I think of the contrast of just hours ago, at that unholy place in the suburbs I call home, where I clean up dog poop and cat throw-up, and argue with my son about everything teenagers like to argue about — which is, everything. I feel a large hole in the heel of my nylon, wondering when the tear will cut loose to fulfill its destiny, and run with lightning speed up my leg. I think back to getting ready for this trip, as I ran across the kitchen floor in my nylons, and my nylon stuck to a clump of cooked rice. When I tried to pick it off, I tore a hole in my nylon. I think of home, but not for long.

The Ritz is in the rich heart of modern Los Angeles. It's a secret pocket that reminds us that the class system is alive and, I think, well. I'm glad. My father used to say that all men were indeed created equal, but that some are just a little more equal than others. Here is where the more than equal stay.

The wide, regal hallway just outside The Bar is studded with chandeliers. French doors line the right side of the corridor, allowing friendly sunshine to splash on the guests who meander there. Renaissance paintings are hung on the other side of the hallway. They are mostly portraits. The people in the portraits include men, women, and sometimes, children. In each portrait the noses are too large and the children's heads are too big. It must have been a style of painting back then. I have the sense that the people portrayed are English. Their skin is consistently too white.

When I walk along the corridor to my room, the staff, from highest to lowest, address me with a greeting, acknowledging the time of day: "Good morning"; "Good afternoon"; "Good evening"—maybe, in case I don't know. Perhaps I look confused. They appear to be aware of the class system and don't seem to mind it. They almost seem happy with the clean division, the neat order of it. Maybe the clear definition is a comfort of sorts.

The corridor encircles a garden that is smattered with spots of colorful flowers and tropical ferns, aesthetically arranged to look random and not the least bit premeditated. The garden's spontaneity has been carefully orchestrated. Exotic flowers bloom with a tame wildness. Even though the garden has a civilized air, it does not have the formal stiffness that the pretend-rich or new-rich often display. Guests stroll along the garden path at a leisurely pace. There's no rush, no panic, no hurry. There is no place anyone needs to be quickly. Orchids appear to have just bloomed, and their bold, fresh faces smile widely as guests pass by.

The staff is composed of various ethnic groups, but is most-ly Mexicans. The staff uses words like "pleasure." "It is my pleasure to serve you" is said often. I wonder if they speak this way at home. It doesn't seem consistent with the Latin lifestyle that I'm familiar with. I too am Latin, and am aware of the tendency toward loud, passionate conversation. This conversa-tional style is the opposite, but it rolls off their tongues so naturally that it surely must be how they speak at home, sport-ing a kind of British politeness.

The maids who clean the rooms wear stiffly starched uni-forms in soft pink. Some of the older maids are a bit fat, and look a little out of sync in this color reserved for thin, young girls. Still, it gives a friendly feeling without being too formal, and acknowledges they are female.

The Bar is paneled in dark carved wood, probably mahogany. I sit at a rococo carved table, sipping a glass of expensive Bordeaux, to record, to write the experience. The lamp on my table is made of highly polished wood and is shaped like a vase. I don't turn the lamp on. I feel slightly self-conscious sitting alone and writing in this opulent bar. I also feel eccentric, having written myself into some sort of part in a movie script. I fancy myself eccentrically and interestingly out of place. I feel mysterious looking. Still, I don't want to turn on the light. I don't want to draw undue attention as I sit alone writing. The light in the room is fading, but for now it is enough.

There is a slight disturbance of quiet activity behind me. Two workmen in Ritz uniforms work silently on something electrical in the rich Persian carpet. A few minutes later, my light goes on. They'd seen me writing. It was getting dark. They had anticipated my need for light and forced it on. They didn't want to interrupt me, but they did want me to have light. Telepathic ability must be a prerequisite for employment at The Ritz, or at least the intuitive sensitivity to know what a guest is about to want, and to fulfill each need before it is requested.

A snack tray is brought to my table. It's silver, with three small bowls connected at the center to a tall handle topped by a lion's head, the Ritz logo. The bowls are filled with exotic treats, not the usual fare one finds in usual bars. No pretzels, no orange fish-shaped crackers, no Spanish peanuts. One bowl contains dried pineapple, coconut, and other, unrecognizable, I'm assuming, fruits. Another bowl offers an extensive assortment of exotic nuts, which includes pistachios and macadamias. The third dish caters to the Asian business traveler, with little nuggets of odd-tasting, sesame-covered morsels. They are orange, red, and green. For some reason Oriental snacks are always more colorful than ours. Portrait spotlights come on and illuminate the paintings on the wall. They are mostly paintings of horses. Their noses are too small. The paintings have an airbrushed look, with soft edges defining subtle shapes. This airbrushed effect was created before airbrushing tools existed. The horses look gracious, courteous, and well mannered, a far cry from the unruly stable horses I ride for $15 an hour.

Two couples who are more important than the rest come into The Bar and are seated personally by the manager. A slight but respectable fuss is made over them. They are served better snacks than I got. A cocktail server attends to them immediately. The cocktail servers are women and are dressed in French maid uniforms in the no-nonsense colors of black and white. The skirts are not short, they are appropriately knee length. The manners are appropriate. The decor is appropriate. Everything around me is appropriate, but surprisingly, not boringly so.

As I sit in The Bar, people come and go. No one stays too long. Except for me.

I'm glad there are still places like this, places of discreet inequity. Nothing is, after all, really equal in this funny little world. To pretend it is, is to be dishonest. I'm bored with the dishonesty I see daily, and am refreshed by The Ritz. It's an honest place, pretending to be nothing other than what it is, a place that is not for everyone, a fancy place for fancy people. And, on occasion, me.

Chapter 3

TANGO ~ THE DANCE OF LOVE

The dance of love, of passion, of heartbreak. Partners dance with no daylight between them. They move as one. In this dance of love, we are dipped, we spin, we are thrown away and brought back. Sometimes, in the intricate steps of love, we fall, or are dropped. We step on toes. Our toes are stepped on. Yet, we continue to be infatuated with this dance more than any other.

SHORT STORY

He was a short story.
And in the end,
not a very interesting one.

When I first met him,
he looked like a novel,
but my own hope
tricked me.

VALENTINE'S DAY, 1998

Dear Heather, How are you? I hope you had a nice Valentine's
Day. Mine pretty much sucked. I broke up with my boyfriend in
December, and was feeling happy with my decision until the full
moon came out of hiding on Valentine's Day. I started drinking
wine with my cleaning guy, Raul, at about 2:00 in the afternoon.
At 3:00 I made him dance flamenco with me in the kitchen. At
4:30 I called my old boyfriend and asked him if he thought his
new girlfriend would mind if I joined them for dinner. He said,
yes, he thought she would mind. At 5:30 I called Mom, who's
seventy-two, and asked her if she wanted to go dancing. She said,
"Sure." That's what we did. Mom and I went dancing at a kind of
disco place. (I didn't know they still had those.) We danced all
night, sometimes with each other, sometimes by ourselves, and
sometimes with some other lonely soul, also out alone, on Valentine's Day night.

Well, I got through another Valentine's Day and, not count-
ing the fairly large hangover I had the next day, I'd say it went
rather well.

THE NEAR-LOVE EXPERIENCE.

He was beautiful.
He was tall, dark,
and, of course, handsome.
He made my heart flutter
and take wing.

I met him at a party.
The room was crowded with people.
I had the feeling
of floating above everyone.
I could hear them talking,
but I wasn't a part of it.

It was
a near-love experience.

As I started to drift off
toward the light,
something kept pulling me back.
It was sanity.

I've been in love before
and it is
a form of insanity,
delicious, delectable
insanity.

I wanted to continue on
toward the beautiful light
that beckoned me,
but alas,
I had more to accomplish
in reality first.
I came back.

Still,
I know it's out there,
love.

And one day,
I shall have it,
giving up sanity
entirely.

The Booger

One day my ex-husband
made me mad.
Actually, what he did was
hurt my feelings,
because hurt in me shows like
mad.

He was an accountant,
and displays of anger
made him uncomfortable.

I stuffed my anger
for a while.

That night
when we went to bed,
I put a booger on his pillow.

The next day
he went to a board meeting
with a booger in his hair.

My anger went away.

SEX WITH THE WRONG MAN

You know right away,
before it technically begins,
this is the wrong man.

But it's too late,
you're committed.
You're there and you're naked.
It would be inappropriate
to jump up,
get dressed,
and say,
"I've changed my mind."

You want to be polite,
and manners do count
in sex.

He begins.
You feel
like a pink tulip
in a field of dry, brown hay.

You can hardly see yourself,
the hay is so tall.
You, in your pinkness,
are in the wrong
place.

The wrong landscape
surrounds you,
drowns you.

Then, suddenly,
you start to enjoy
this touch,
that caress.

Your stem starts to stretch
toward the sky.
You grow tall.
You find yourself
growing taller than the wheat,
which turns to
a rich green.

It tries to match your height,
but you're growing too fast.

Your pink petals start to open, wide.
Your petals spread their wings,
and reach
heaven.

You explode,
throwing pieces of pinkness
across the landscape.

And then,
you are happy.
You bathe in your own pinkness
and
in him.

And you realize,
this time,
it was not
sex with the wrong man.
Not this time.
Not this man.

THE PYRAMID

My beliefs were neatly stacked in the shape of a pyramid. This was my belief system.

The most basic, truest beliefs were the bottom stones of the pyramid. These stones were big and solid, forming the foundation of everything I knew to be true. These beliefs consisted of: "God is good," "The world is round," and "Love is never-ending."

The secondary stones were one level up. They were less important beliefs, but also true. These beliefs included: I am a secretary. I don't jog. I like birds, but I'd never own one because they're messy.

The stones on the next level up were small and could be changed or eliminated entirely without affecting the foundation of the belief system. These smaller beliefs were: My favorite color is blue. My hair is brown. I use Maybelline makeup.

When he left, telling me he didn't love me anymore, one of the foundation stones, "love is never-ending," was pulled out. It was a big stone. With one of the primary stones gone, all the other stones came tumbling down. All my beliefs lay piled in a disheveled heap. My pyramid had crumbled. I had crumbled.

The remaining foundation stones needed to be reassessed to see if they too were lies. I didn't know what to believe. I didn't know what was true anymore. I asked myself if indeed God was good, and if the world was really round.

Time passed and wounds began to heal. After careful and hysterical consideration, I accepted that God was good and the world was probably round. I began to rebuild. I changed my favorite color to purple, opened an advertising agency, started jogging, died my hair red, bought a parrot, and began to wear Christian Dior makeup. This did not happen overnight. But it did happen.

Since then, I have added a new foundation stone. I now believe we get stuck in our belief systems. And God brings us chaos, and sometimes pain, offering us the opportunity to re-align ourselves, to reinvent ourselves into a brighter, newer, fresher version of who we are, sloughing off crusty old dreams and weary perceptions.

Oh, and I still believe love is never-ending. But it's my loving, not necessarily theirs.

SHINY BLACK NIGHT

You bring my world
back into awe,
as I once knew it
through innocent eyes.

Deep blue mysteries,
that I thought
had vanished,
reappear.

Shiny black night
creates silhouettes
against luminous pink clouds.

The little girl in me
comes out to play
couched safely
in your strength.

When I stand
beside you,
the moon is bigger,
the stars shine brighter.

Demons dance,
then disappear,

and God speaks more gently
than ever before.

My heart peeks out
and softly explodes.

New textures.
New dimensions.
New levels of laughter.

The deep, rich sound
of your voice
melts me.

And more God rays
shine through
smoky clouds
than ever the earth
has seen.

THE DECISION

A friend told me a story about a man who left his wife. He found someone else, younger, cuter, and, I'm sure, thinner.

After shedding many tears, the wife pulled herself together and began to date. She met a very nice man and they began to date. Some months later, her soon to be ex-husband wanted her back. He told her in no uncertain terms that she had to decide immediately who she wanted to be with. She said, "No, I don't have to decide right now and I won't decide until I know."

This was a remarkable story for me, as I never knew "indecision" was an option. I didn't know there were three choices available with an ultimatum. Now that I do, I think it will come in handy. (And ... I heard that, eventually, when she was ready, she chose the new guy.)

GOOD THINGS TO SAY TO BAD MEN

1. "Get out!"

2. "It's plain to see you're used to dealing with stupid women." (For some reason, this one really makes men mad.)

3. The scene: You're waiting for his call. It doesn't come. Finally, you call him.

   "Hi, were you going to call me?"

   "Oh. Why, yes."

   "Good." (Click!)

4. "I don't think you're afraid of commitment; I think you're an emotional sissy."

STILLNESS

I am in a time
of stillness.

No old lovers calling.
No one pining for me.
No new lovers
surprising me
with their calls.

Silence.

I wonder
if a cauldron
is boiling
somewhere,
beneath the stillness,
giving birth to

new adventures,
new loves,
new passions,
still to come.

THE RHYTHM

We dance.
I follow your steps.
It is my nature to follow.

Am I a slave to your steps?
In a sense, yes.
In a nobler sense,
no.

They are,
after all,
just steps.

We continue to dance
as our dance becomes
wild,
passionate,
beautiful.

Then one day...
The rhythm inside you
changes,
slowly.
I don't feel the changing,
and when it happens,
it feels
abrupt.

And so,
a new dance begins.

I trip at first,
my feet unaccustomed
to the new rhythm.

This new dance is different.
I don't cling to you
as once I did.
No longer
do you dip me downward,
hovering above me,
holding me,
not letting me fall.

I was safe
then.

Perhaps this new dance
will have
grand sweeping twirls
accompanied
by a different kind of laughter.

Can this new rhythm
sustain the dance?
Will my feet
be able to accommodate
the new steps,
which still
seem so awkward?
Can I follow you
gracefully
in this new rhythm?

I don't know.

If only I could
turn off the old rhythm
that still
beats so strongly
in my heart.

FLYING

He always kept his feet
firmly on the ground.
I had the tendency
to fly
too high.

I married him,
thinking
he would help me
keep my feet
on the ground.

Then one day,
he left.

With my wings no longer
bound to my sides,
I flew very, very high.
It was
wondrous.

I was surprised to find
that as high as I flew,
I had never been
in any actual danger.

THE KIND OF WHORE I AM

I am:

~ A compliment whore.
   Someone pays me a compliment and my legs automatically spring open.

~ A travel whore.
   Offer me a trip to an exotic land and see what happens.

~ A word whore.
   Speak the English language beautifully and with articulation and I'm yours.

~ A French accent whore.
   Say anything at all to me in French (I don't speak French, so it doesn't matter what you say), and let the fun begin.

I am on occasion:

~ A jewelry whore.
   But only if the guy's handsome and I love him and the jewelry's big.

~ A beautiful new home whore.
   But only with the above stipulations—handsome and I must love him.

However, let it be known that I never do whoring with my soul, not ever.

CUMBERSOME

The cumbersome stage. The beginning. The start of an unknown path. All encompassing. Swallowing me. Maybe swallowing him too.

Each day finds one of us tipping the scale. The next day it changes partners. Who likes whom better and by how much? Eating moves to the second rung of survival. A mysterious passion ribbons into first place, unknown, never to be understood. Only its strong, undeniable presence announces its existence. It's here. It's big.

We share times of yellow daffodil-like joy, with uproarious laughter, and succulent moments of deep secrets exchanged lightly, as if they were feathers. And mountains of sweet, hot loving.

There are also unstoppable times of troublesome insecurities that come out of hiding and bash the happy times. They come from the springboard of nothing. Fighting occurs. Arguments ensue. No one is prepared. It is always a surprise. The joy is covered by a thick, black goo.

And then, just as suddenly, for no apparent reason, the thick blackness slides off, revealing a glimmer of the yellow joy and pink sweetness. We talk. We explain. We apologize. We are okay again. The remembering of old hurts goes back to its hiding place. The shabby, antique pain sleeps once more. And so, it seems, the story cannot be rushed and insists on being told at its own pace, in its own time.

The dilemma, however, continues. How much to tell? How much to hide? How straight to stand in my own circle, how deep to fall into his? How lost will I be? How lost is he? It is a game designed to be played by two. One player alone is simply a daydream. I must be careful that I am not in a daydream.

Attempts to measure the other heart continue. It is done blindly, awkwardly. There is no gauge to measure the depth of the beloved's heart. Equal speeds must also be maintained. It is important to fall at the same speed. My fall is partially determined by my falling partner's speed — but only partially. There should be a rope tying us together, regulating our speed, to avoid danger, equalizing the speeding fall so that no one should hurry forward, no one should lag behind.

Client copy sits unwritten while I compose love poems.

And then, one day the cumbersome phase is over. And if we are especially lucky, and the gods are in a generous mood, determining that we remain together, we will remember these times with a longing to return to the sweet ache of this cumbersome ... magic.

EMPTY

I cannot be with you
any longer.

You steal me,
leaving me,
empty.

AFTER THE DIVORCE

After the divorce, she met Jon.
When they made love,
she would cry and couldn't stop.
She felt like she was cheating
on someone,
but didn't know whom.

Poor Jon.

FOREVER

He said,
he would love me
forever.
His forever
was shorter
than mine.

THE SOFA

When he left me,
it was like someone
had pulled the living room rug
out from under me.
My furniture and I
were tossed into the air.

When the furniture landed,
it came down in a new,
more interesting arrangement
that actually suited me better.
And I landed on the soft sofa.

CLASSIFIED AD

Wanted: The Cake
Requested By: The Icing

Cool, fluffy icing, looking for a cake. I hardly ever cook, and
when I do it's pretty bad. My son says, "If it's not frozen, we don't
eat it." I'm also not especially neat. But I can introduce you to
strange, exotic music you've never heard before. I can teach you
to knock over a lighter on the floor with just your nose. I don't
usually say the right things at corporate functions, but I can show
you the common strands in all the religions of the world. I

can't tell you what Congress or the Senate does, but I can teach you how to count to ten in Balinese.

I don't have a clue as to how electricity works, and sometimes I get right and left mixed up. I don't understand why pay phones can't give change but cigarette machines can, or why people find it so hard to love one another. I don't understand why Ireland is fighting with itself, or why the Israelis are fighting with the Palestinians. I do, however, understand that God exists, and is called by many different names. I've heard it said, that "Science trying to prove the existence of God would be like humans trying to prove math to dogs." I agree.

So, if you can show me how to be appropriate at corporate parties, help me out with right and left, and give me a brief explanation of electricity, then I'll show you how to see the aura of a tree, and how to love with your heart fully open.

And together, we just might make a beautiful pastry.

IRONY

A friend of mine was asked
by a guy she was dating,
if she was dating him
for his money.

She told him
he didn't have enough.

She then asked him
if he was dating her
for her body.
He said yes.

NOT READY

If he leaves you,
and you're not ready,
just tell him,
"Wait!
I haven't fallen out of love with you yet."

DRUNKEN MOON

Driving home
beneath a drunken moon,
you come into my mind
like a shooting star.
"We" are done,
but sadly,
I am not.

The crescent moon
slips behind the clouds
and then peeks out again,
like memories of you.

You are
the mystery unsolved,
the book unfinished,
the canvas partially painted.
I was not done with you,
as you became done with me.
My relentless yearning for you
aches.

During the day's sunny brightness,
the longing for you hides.
In the light of day
you vanish.

But, alas,
it is night.

Mystical, magical music
fills my car as you dance in my head.
Mystical, magical moon
plays hide-and-seek
with the night clouds,
bringing you
once again
to me.

You bring me to weakness
as I have never felt before,
making me stronger
than I have ever been before.

When did weakness
begin to taste so sweet?
When did my heart
learn to beat
so deeply?

How can
even the pain for you
be so delicious?

When did
the giving up of power
begin to feel
so powerful?

Am I willing
to give up
this feeling of pain
so sharp,
for feelings
of nothingness?

Please,
come to me again completely,
or leave me completely,
so I can
once again
live
without feeling
cheated.

MISSING PARTS

We are each other's
nonessential
missing parts.

I can function
without you,
but not quite
so richly.

Like a color
missing
from the rainbow.

IMPRINT

You will be with me
forever.
You have been imprinted
upon my soul.
I am branded by you.

No matter what happens,
this will always be true.
No matter how things seem to be,
this will always be true.

It will be true
beyond life.
If there are other lives,
I will carry your imprint on me
even there.

You penetrate me
like yellow rays of the sun,
forever staining my skin.

The sweet, mushy sentimentality
of my feelings for you
will still exist,
from you,
with you,
in me,
far beyond
the world's scanty definition
of forever.

Can I ever leave you?
No, not really.

Even when it looks as though I do,
the imprint of you
remains.

You
remain.

SALARY

He boasted to her
that he pulled in a
six-figure salary.

She asked him
if that included
the decimal point.

PEPTO-BISMOL

Before I go on a blind date, I eat two chewable Pepto-Bismol tablets. The chemical, bismuth, in Pepto-Bismol makes a person's tongue black.

At the end of the evening, if I don't want to kiss the guy, I yawn widely, making sure he can see my tongue. Once he's seen my tongue, there's not a snowball's chance in hell he'll try to kiss me.

If I do like the guy, I simply keep my mouth shut. Trust me, girls, this works.

THE SCALE

On a scale of
1 to 10
I saw him as
a 4,000.

He saw himself
as a 3.

That's the level on
which he operated —
a 3.

I thought I could help him

to see himself as
at least
a 4.

He never did.
He left me.

I made him nervous.
4,000 was too high,
4 was too high.

Too bad.

Rust-Oleum

He was a sensitive man.
To prevent himself
from getting hurt
he would occasionally
turn his feelings
off.

One time
he was hurt very badly,
and left his feelings
off
too long.

Like a rusty faucet,
his feelings
got stuck
in the off position.

He no longer felt pain.
He no longer felt joy.
He hadn't realized
that hurt and happiness

were connected to
the same valve.

One day,
she came into his life.
She had a big jar
of rust solvent.
She unstuck him
and he never shut off
again.

He knew now
it was
dangerous.

CRUSTED HEART

Excuse me, sir,
but my heart
has become hard
and crusted over.

You know,
for protection.

It has been wounded.

I had a flit of a feeling
when I met you,
that your tender fingers
could knead it back
to its once pliable softness
of pink bubble gum.

It was just a feeling I had
about you
and about me.

WILD AND SPUNKY

I considered myself
a wild, worldly,
interesting woman,
full of spunk.
I was fun
and spicy —
the kind of woman
men left their suburbanite
wives for.

We met.
We fell in love.
We married.

Then, one day,
he left me.
for a suburbanite wife.

APART

We were already
apart.

I just recognized it first
and did the leaving.

THE ONLY ONE

I guess,
in the end,
it wasn't that
you didn't love me
enough.

You didn't love you
enough.

And I couldn't be
the only one
loving you.

CANDY

You are brightly colored candy behind the glass of a candy jar.
For a long time I tried to break the glass to be with you. You
looked so good, so sweet and tasty. You had so many bright, de-
licious-looking colors. But the glass was too strong. I couldn't
break it. You remained inside the glass. I remained outside, looking in. Then, for a time, I was content to just look at you through
the glass, to be near you, without touching you.

Now, I'm not content with candy I can't have. I want candy I
can touch, hold, and taste. I want all the stickiness, all the sweetness that candy can offer. I want to lick it and roll it around on
my tongue. I want to taste love.

And that I shall have. No longer will I accept love behind
a glass.

WHISTLING

It is virtually impossible
to whistle
while making love.

I have discovered, however,
that one can
laugh
while making love.

I do not, however,
recommend doing this.

Your partner
will not be amused.

FLIGHT PATH

The crickets burped
through the summer night.

Children's voices echoed
off the hot asphalt street.

Craggy mountains
reached high
as I reached
my fiftieth year.

An arrogant,
black silky night
swept over me.

Perhaps a detour,
perhaps a sign
of beginnings,
of newer, grander,
slicker adventures
to come.

As this night blew over me,
old nights of half-eaten lobster tails
and empty green wine bottles
seemed silly.

This night brought
odd concerts in Berkeley

by people I'd never heard of,
and bicycling fast down hills
on sunny days.

This night held secrets.
As the secrets peeked
above the horizon,
spring showed itself
in a pallet of pastels.

Slick, black night
tasted the pastels
and enjoyed
the sweetness.

In my fiftieth year
I watched him taste,
and I came upon
my own juncture.

Open,
unknowingness,
confusion and delight.

And then
we let go.

And so it was
black night
and me,
each went
on our own journey.

From time to time,
holding hands
when we happened to be
on the same flight path.

CLOSET SPACE

Longing for you
for so long
has become
a bore.

The memories of you
no longer
justify
the closet space.

LEFT

When my husband left me
I stopped writing.
I didn't know
what was true anymore.

I could commit nothing
to ink
or even
to pencil.

Time has passed
and I'm pleased to report
I can now write
in indelible
ink.

REFLECTION

No longer
can you use
my eyes
to reflect back

to you
your beauty.

The moment has come
for you to shine
through your own
eyes.

I must go now
and find my own
reflection.

But
know this
before I go—
the reflection of you
that shone
through my eyes
is true.

You are beautiful.
Just look long and deep
and you too
will see it.

And one day,
if we are lucky,
we will meet again.

And shine outward
our own reflections
to each other.

STOPPED

He stopped loving me
in the thick of my
loving him.

He was finished,
but I was not.

I felt like I had been stopped
in the middle of an orgasm.

TWILIGHT IN TOBAGO

Palm trees glisten from the moon's touch on a high grassy cliff
silhouetted by the sea. The sky begins to sink. On this wild tropical island night I wear a long, loose-fitting dress of white gauze.
It sways with each movement of the ocean breeze, caressing my
tanned body.

My husband of not many months is with me. Our marriage is
new. We are new. We do not speak. There is too much to feel.

On this warm, humid night, we are cooled by waves crashing
on the rocks below as the sea splashes us with droplets of itself.
We are exposed and open. We do not remember ever having
been closed. As the sky is swallowed by the night, it leaves a bold
wake of orange and red strewn randomly across the night's canvas. Strong brush strokes of opposing colors meet and bleed
into each other. The sea is deep and purple. It is wild and free...
as we are.

Palm fronds rustle to the rhythm of the wind, creating mysterious music in the darkness. Lights from a distant freighter
throw tiny lines of brightness across the sea's jagged surface. We
can see, but are not seen.

The closing of the day on this cliff overlooking the turbulent
sea brings abandonment. The feeling is weightless and lofty. At

this moment in time, I am, he is, as the wild sea, innocent and true.

SINGLE IN THE '80S

(*Written in 1988*)

I'm thirty-nine, and have been divorced for nine years. I have no answers, but would like to explore the questions.

It seems to me that men are losing their penises and women are growing them.

I was independent, and I loved my husband. He left me. I had to learn to do things for myself. I became more independent through necessity. Now, men don't seem to like this independence or know what to do with it. They seem scared, though I don't know why. To venture a guess, it seems a mighty number of men are so scared that they don't have a penis, that they might as well not have one.

My group is the ex-hippies. We were idealistic about world love. Then we got jobs. We became CPAs, doctors, lawyers. Got money, got things, filled our lives with stuff. Then, I guess we missed the idealism and got idealistic about one-on-one love. We left our husbands, left our wives. They weren't perfect. Where did we ever get the idea that "perfect love" meant the loving of someone "perfect?" Who told us that marriage would be, could be, perfect? Who gave us this childish notion? What about the loyalty and longevity of loving? Where did that go? Wouldn't it be sad if I were the only one left who believed in that. I'd have no receiver to give it to.

The majority of men I meet seem to be emotional sissies. They got hurt once. Who hasn't? Big deal. So what? Boohoo, a woman might try to take a man's money. Well, guess what? She just might want something more costly than his money—like his love. Sadly, this rarely occurs to the majority.

Maybe faith isn't meant to be directed only to God. Maybe faith is for us to have for each other, too. We use a huge word like faith for God and a tiny little concept like trust for ourselves. Faith is all encompassing; trust is simply falling backward and hoping that someone will catch you.

Women are waiting for Romeos, but they're not Juliets. Men are waiting for Cleopatras, but they're not Anthonys. Work is our love now, our passion. We work overtime. It has become normal time. We work hard. We play hard. We schedule our play as we schedule business appointments. We perform play with such forced intensity that it has lost its fun, its spontaneity. No one's really relaxed anymore.

We're too fat or too skinny, too old or too young, our boobs too small or too big. Everything is "too" something, not perfect. Personally, I think perfection would be a major drag, boring. We jog. We run. I wonder to or from what. We want to have bodies like twenty-year-olds. We already did.

I don't terribly mind changing a tire if I have to. I like a man changing a tire for me even better. I like depending on a man. I do not find these desires mutually exclusive. There are many things a man can do better than me. I like that. I like them being bigger and having more body hair. I like that they don't cry as easily as I do. I love all the differences. I don't want to be a man. I have never envied a penis. I like what I have.

I would love nothing more than to love a man, but I will survive and change a tire if one's not around. I've had to learn to do that. It wasn't anything I purposely set out to learn; I just had to because there was no one to do it for me. And now, I like the fact that I can. I want to be a little girl to a man. I want to be a sexy woman to a man. I want to be his best friend and help him change a tire. I wonder what's so scary about all that.

Too Busy To Be Lonely—
Single in the Year 2000

When I tell someone I'm lonely, their usual response is, "I'm too busy to be lonely." This makes absolutely no sense to me.

Like everyone else, I have an excruciatingly busy life. Perhaps I'm the only person in the universe who can be busy and lonely at the same time. These are two entirely different subjects. Busy is having a lot of things to do. Lonely is being alone and not feeling okay about it.

I can feel alone and not lonely. I can be with people and feel lonely. They're completely different situations. The kind of lonely I feel is the man-woman, romantic kind. I feel the need to be part of a couple, part of a team of two. I want to find my "other half." And before those of you who might be tempted say that I *am* complete without a man, let me say that I have considered this, and have come to the conclusion that God gave me these feelings, which are instinctive, for the purpose, I suppose, of propagating the species. Although my days of propagation are long gone, I'm still left with remnants of these instinctive tendencies, which should perhaps have waned by now. In any case, they haven't. Any kind of trendy, modern style of thinking that attempts to deny these God-given instincts is just . . . denial.

I have had love. I have been a part of a couple. I liked it. I know there are people who have had a bad marriage or two or three, and would never consider hooking up with a partner again. I'm not one of those people. My relationships, like all relationships, did not consist only of perpetual sweetness and light. There were, of course, times of trouble, and yet I liked "working *on* a relationship" better than "working *at finding* a relationship."

I have plenty of wonderful friends, both male and female. I'm not short of love in the general sense, and I'm not looking for someone to "save me" or buy me a new house. I have a loving and terrific son. I own my own business, which is fairly successful. I have a small but well-decorated house, good health, a loving family, and am in good physical shape. I am so, so appreciative of these things, and yet I still find myself lonely. Lonely for a partner.

I am sad to say that I am particularly picky about whom I'm willing to couple up with, which, of course, makes it harder. I didn't choose this harder path, I just find myself on it. As I get older I have a smaller market to choose from. I go into battle with fewer weapons, skin not so taut, body not as shapely as it once was. Men I wouldn't have even glanced at when I was younger now reject me. I fear I will become bitter toward men. I don't want that to happen, yet I sense feelings of bitterness encroaching.

I do the right things, go to the right places, make myself visible and accessible, yet here I am on a beautiful Saturday, writing about loneliness. I feel like I'm in a game of musical chairs. There are only a few chairs left, the music is winding down, and I'm not even close to a chair.

I went into hibernation one year. I had decided to pout. I became invisible. I avoided men. I'd heard all my life that you get what you're *not* looking for. Well, I've proven that wrong. I got nothing. I became invisible, and indeed, no one saw me.

I have a few girlfriends who admit that they too are lonely. Others don't seem to be, or at least won't admit it. They fill their lives by remodeling their homes, being way too involved in the lives of their grown children, or just hanging out with their girlfriends. They seem to have found other things to replace what, I'm certain, they must really want. I've tried to do this and have had short-lived, sporadic success. I've spent too much of my life learning to be honest with myself about what I'm feeling, and I fear it's too late for me to go into denial, as tempting as it looks.

I am invisible where once I was seen, at times, even shone. My hormones are all over the place. Can I blame it all on that?

It would be nice, but probably not. I still have so much to give, yet there is no one to give it to. I am a tree falling in the forest, with no one to hear the sound of my crash. What do I do with all this? Where do I put it? Whom do I give it to?

I have always been a fairly happy person. I don't like this unhappy person I am becoming. There's an underlying current of discontentment and disillusionment.

So, I've defined the problem, looking it square in the face. Maybe defining the problem will help. I hope.

August 2002 — Update

I feel like I'm in love. And no one's around.

I don't mean to sound sappy, but, like someone in love, I'm sure I will. I feel whole and grounded in a way I've never experienced before. I have, somehow, accidentally bumped into a new texture of love that I never knew existed. It's strange and wondrous.

There's nothing magically new in my life, except that I'm writing a book. Writing it seriously. Writing it for publication. I'm willing to fail hugely. I'm willing to succeed hugely. What I'm not willing to do is to not try. I am not willing to have a book inside me that does not get published.

I've spent most of my life looking for approval from others and validation from men in the form of romance. I now seek my own approval, and it's a glorious feeling. I feel freer than I have ever felt before. I've learned to be kind to myself. I am finally allowing myself the freedom to be the many forms of me that I am.

Like most women, I've taken care of people all my adult life. I've spent a good part of my life caring for others: family, friends, clients, bosses, and a husband. Now I'm taking care of myself with the same love I've bestowed on others. This is not to the exclusion of others, but in addition.

I've spent the past twenty years as a single woman trying to be a married woman again. This wasn't necessarily an unworthy goal. But I now believe the way I viewed the goal was. I was looking to fix what I felt was broken—a failed marriage. I thought I needed a Band-Aid to cover the wound and carry on, with my new man, my new love, giving me justification for the break that had occurred. I figured that a new man, a new marriage, a new coupling, would make everything okay again. It never happened.

I've had my share of grand loves that enriched my life in so many ways. Every one of them was a delicious experience, bringing me all the wild and delirious adventures that love brings. Yet, I never remarried. Perhaps there was no Band-Aid big enough.

I'm happy now, happy not to have the insatiable hunger I've had for so long. Being alone now feels like a nice, clean closet, free of clutter. I have found love. I've found it in my writing. This is not a better love. It is a different love, a love for this moment in time. This love, too, is grand. It's as wide as my arms can open, and not in the least bit exclusive. It is for everyone.

And one day, if I am lucky, and a sweet gossamer breeze is blowing in the right direction, and God deems it so, I shall have romantic love again. For now, I have this ... and I feel like I'm in love.

Chapter 4

FLAMENCO ~ THE MISCELLANEOUS STUFF FROM WHICH LIFE IS MADE

lamenco is the dance of fire and ice. It can start slow and pensive and in an instant turn wild and furious. As the dancer dances, she looks down, dancing for herself, lost in her own reflection. Each movement carries an implosion of feelings too large to hold inside, demanding release and exploding outward into physical expression. In the midst of her dance, she looks up, almost surprised to see an audience. She stares out for just a moment, then looks down again, dismissing the audience, and continues on with her dance, absorbed in the moment, nestled deep within herself. The audience is irrelevant. It's the dance that matters.

Flamenco is a dance that is wholly and purely art. And like art, it is almost beyond definition. It is a form of art requiring courage, discipline, dignity, humor, and freedom, much like the art of life. And like the art of life, it encompasses supreme moments of joy, despair, passion, ecstasy, delight, sorrow, and, ultimately, hope.

LATE IN THE MORNINGS

I get to work late
most every morning.
I dance naked
in front of my full-length mirror.

Sometimes I dance hot and fiery
with wild abandon
to the passion of
the flamenco guitar.

Sometimes light and airy
to the exotic sounds
of trance music.
Sometimes I dance
flirtatiously
and sensually
to Arabian music.
Always, the music is loud.

Sometimes I dance
with Baby, my cockatoo,
on my shoulder.
Sometimes I accommodate
her presence
and restrict my movements
so she won't fall.
Sometimes I don't,
and she just has to hang on.

My morning dancing is
the most nonproductive,
apparently useless,
apparently vain,

apparently self-indulgent
thing I can do.

It is the most spirited
thing I do.

It reminds me who I was
before I started
"belonging"
to people.

It reminds me that,
ultimately,
I belong to myself.

I give exercise to the
flowing, graceful spirit
that is, sadly,
most times,
caged
and behaving properly.

Precious wild moments
out of the cage.
My dearest part,
play,
play wildly.

You are succinctly me.
My heartbeat.
My talent.
My beauty.
My grace.
Everything in me,
wild.
Everything in me,
free.

Caging hurts,
but must be.
You are not allowed to play
in front of others.

Be happy, most precious part,
I love you.
And will always
let you out.

I will be
late in the mornings,
and you will
dance wildly,
naked.

BEAUTIFUL

She never knew
how beautiful
her eyes shone
in the sunlight.

She could not see
her own eyes.

Other people
could,
but no one had
ever told her.

One day, on a train,
someone did
and she cried.

WHEN TIME STANDS STILL

If you want to know
what's important in your life,
pay attention
to what you're doing
when time
stands still.

Whatever you're doing
when time stops
is very, very important,
giving you a road map
to your destiny.

For me, it's writing
and, of course, making love,
sometimes physically,
but always
when I'm making love
happen.

FLYING

I often dream that I'm flying.
It is exhilarating.

In the dream,
I see people below me
walking around.

I tell them
to come and fly with me.
Without looking up,
they say,
"No one can fly."

I tell them,
"Look up,
I'm flying.
You can fly too."

But they won't look up.
They just continue
to shake their heads, saying,
"No one can fly."

I leave them
and continue flying,
going as fast and high
as I can.

Then, I wake up
and the same thing
happens in real life.

KILTER

What is a "kilter,"
and how do we know
when we're
off it?

DESPERATION

I've seen
lives of quiet desperation.

For myself, I prefer
my desperation
loud and obvious.

THE PLAYGROUND

We hold on tightly
to the monkey bars,
knowing
that if we fall
we will land
in a swamp full of alligators.
When we do fall,
we find it was
just soft sand.

Sometimes, when we swing,
we fall
hard.
We cry
hard.

Then we get up
and swing
again.

Some of us don't
get back on the swing.

Sometimes, when we're high
on the end of the seesaw,
the other guy gets off
and we bump to the ground.
Some of us get back on the seesaw,
wanting to feel that high spot again.
Others don't.

Sometimes, someone pushes us on the swing.
Sometimes, we swing ourselves.
In both cases,
it's possible to fall.

It's also possible to swing very high
and spread our toes,
feeling the wind between them.

Sometimes, we play with other kids.
Sometimes, they hit us and run away.
Sometimes, they kiss us
and stay.

Sometimes, everyone on the playground
is mean.
Other times,
they're nice.

Sometimes, it rains
and we have to go
home.

THE COLOR OF GOODNESS

Goodness comes in different colors.
Pink goodness
is the most common.
It is sweet and airy and gentle,
and has the sound
of a wind chime.

There's also yellow goodness,
which has a high pitch,
and shoots out like a ray.

Then there's purple goodness,
which is my personal favorite.
It's strong and true,
and usually quite profound.
This is a happiness with substance.

It tends to be rich and thick,
and has a very deep sound,
like, I imagine,
the voice of God.
Often, you don't recognize it
as goodness until later,
and when you do,
you realize it was goodness
of a huge magnitude.

Sometimes I go through a period
where I feel like I've been
too good too long.
This simply means
I've been swimming around
in too much goodness
of the sugary, pink kind.
Too much
of this kind of happiness
can feel like a toothache.
I quickly switch to purple
and feel much better.

HURT AND HAPPINESS

If the hurt
in your life
doesn't feel as bad
as the happiness
feels good,
you're on the right track.
Keep doing
what you're doing.

Haiku without the Right Number of Syllables

Massive sunset of flaming orange
strewn across the sky.
Beautiful.
Words
to describe it
awkward.
Like trying to paint
a Monet
with a crayon.

Another Haiku

A bell rings in the night
making
silver ripples
in the dark silence.

Looking for Love

I've spent my life
looking for love.

I thought it would come
in the form
of a man.

And some of it
did.

THE NUMBER COLLECTOR

She collected numbers. Odd numbers, even numbers, and, of course, fractions. She used the numbers to know who she was and where she was.

She had eaten 219 Popsicles in her life, 53 of them were cherry. She was 45 years old. She weighed 130 pounds. She had 15 nail polishes, 4 were frosted. One time she tried to count her eyelashes, but it was too hard. She had been single for 17 years and had had 15 boyfriends, averaging less than 1 per year: 2 were highly intelligent, 4 were stupid as a stick, 3 had great cars, 4 were great lovers, and 2 were not noteworthy in any way.

One rainy Monday, she found she couldn't breathe. The numbers were strangling her. Her paint-by-numbers existence was squeezing the life out of her. She came to the painful conclusion that she needed to give up numbers. She decided she would go on a numbers diet. She was scared, but there was no other choice. She would die by the numbers.

At first, life without numbers was frightening. She didn't know how to live a life that was not clearly and succinctly defined by numbers. They had been her constant companions, her reference to all things and to herself. She wasn't used to life without borders.

One sunny Tuesday, after having been on the numbers diet for a week, she realized that everything she saw, everything she knew, had changed. Her life had taken on a numberless quality. Life without reference felt boundless. She felt free. Everything she saw looked fresh. Even familiar old things looked new, including herself. As boundaries disappeared, the world became vast and randomly beautiful. She felt floaty and unrestrained, like she wasn't wearing underwear.

She didn't have an age. She didn't weigh any pounds. She didn't remember how many lovers she'd had or how many cherry Popsicles she had eaten.

She knew, now, that life was too abundant, too beautiful, to be contained by numbers ... and so was she.

GOAL

My biggest
goal in life
has been to find one.

BUMPS

I like to wear
my insides,
outside.
Then someone
bumps up against them
and I go inside again,
but just
for a little while.

THE LINE

Where does the line go
between
self-love and
selfishness,
and how do we know
when we cross it?

LOST AT THE TRAIN STATION

Three times, I've lost valuable items at the train station: my wallet, a credit card, and a beautiful leather briefcase I'd bought in Venice.

Each time, I was sure that one of the homeless people living at the train station, or one of the teenage girls you see hanging around, with hair that's way too black and skin that's way too white, wearing black lipstick and covered with body piercings, would keep my lost item.

Each time, the item was turned in to the train station and returned to me.

Who started the rumor that the world is not full of good people anymore? There are good people everywhere. Just open your eyes and you'll see them. Even at train stations.

GAUGES

Feelings are gauges.

If something feels good
and comes from a place
very deep down,
do more of it.
It's a good thing.

If, however,
it feels good,
but comes from
a shallow place,
ignore it.

It's a fake reading,
put there
to make the game
more interesting.

NO MATTER WHAT

No matter what,
keep on living.

GIRL WORDS, BOY WORDS

While playing in her mind one day, she bumped into the words, "courage," "honor," and "integrity." She realized that, as a woman, these words were foreign to her. These were words men used. She hadn't been introduced to these words when she was little. Her heroines never spoke these words in fairy tales. Fairy princesses and her Barbie doll would never have occasion to utter these words. Her brother's toy soldiers, however, would.

As she considered this, she realized that, as a woman, these were words, and moreover, concepts, that could add a new and perhaps rich dimension to her life. As she spoke the words "courage," "honor," and "integrity," she rolled them around on her tongue. They tasted delicious. She decided to keep these man-words and infuse them into her world.

In all fairness, she also considered that men were not given words like "compassion," or "sweetness," or "nurture" when they were little boys. Women, of course, were given these words, often to a fault. She would introduce these girl-words to every man she met. She would have them at least taste these words. Maybe they would like them.

She hoped the rest of her clan would do the same, figuring it was up to each man and each woman to teach the missing words to the opposite sex. And maybe we wouldn't find the opposite sex so opposite after all. And perhaps the best words were never meant to be ... gender specific.

COLORING

If you find yourself
coloring outside the lines
and if this makes you nervous,
make the lines wider.

THE CHIT THEORY

A new scientific theory has recently come to light, which
has been widely accepted as irrefutably true by the entire
scientific community. It's been reported in all the newspapers
and scientific journals.

It's called the "Chit Theory." The theory introduces the
revolutionary new concept that every time someone experiences
happiness, they collect a chit. A happiness chit. The chit is, of
course, invisible. The theory goes on to conclude that he who
lives with the most chits wins. This is touted as the new, true
definition of success.

Based on this new clarification, everyone is eligible for
success, including bag ladies, fat people, poor people, people
who wear clothes that don't match, women who have facial
hair, and men who don't. This theory is applicable to absolutely
everyone, including people whose lives we hadn't thought were
successful at all — until now.

As it turns out, we were taught to define success using the
wrong criteria. Much like when we thought the world was flat,
we have been using the wrong powers of observation. Money is
one of the criteria recently discovered to have nothing at all to
do with actual success. Being beautiful is another. Intelligence can
be fun, but again, not a criterion for success. Many of the people
who have these attributes do not, as it turns out, necessarily have
a lot of happiness chits. As a matter of fact, many of them seem
to be quite lacking in chits.

So, if you've looked at people who are richer, more beautiful, and more intelligent than you, who live in big houses, go to fancy parties, and travel the world, and felt that they were more successful than you, well, that's no longer proven to be a scientific fact.

And if you've been busy collecting happiness chits living in your little house, with your little salary, going to block parties, and taking camping vacations, it's highly probable that you are more successful than many of the rich, intelligent, beautiful people. So, keep doing what you're doing.

Be happy. Be successful. Collect chits.

CRAP

I realized at one point that I have my crap and other people have theirs. When I came to this realization, it became immediately clear what was mine and what was theirs. I could actually see the crap line.

I decided that I would not cross that line, and I would not permit anyone else to cross the line either. I would not give them my crap and I would not take their crap.

Now, when someone tries to give me their crap, I refuse it. I have enough of my own. And every now and then, when I inadvertently try to give them mine, I immediately catch myself, apologize, and take mine back.

As it turns out, everybody's crap is custom designed, and it doesn't really fit well on other people.

EYEGLASSES

You've probably noticed
that when you're happy,
and look behind you,
it feels like
you've always been happy,
and when you look in front of you,
it feels like
you will always be happy.

When you're sad, same thing:
you're sad now,
you've always been sad,
and you will be sad forever.

It's like you're looking
through a pair of
happy or sad glasses,
and everywhere you look,
you see
what you're feeling
at that moment.

So, be cautious
of feelings
that wear glasses,
they can be
tricky.

ON THE TRAIN

I ride on the train,
sipping Chardonnay
poured from a miniature bottle
as I watch the scenery go by.

A realization lands on me.

I am also a part of
the beautiful, moving landscape.
Sister to:
flapping white gull wings
against a flat blue sky;
rippling seaweed,
the ocean's hair,
flowing gently
with the current's soft breeze;
a puppy's soft tongue licking my cheek,
leaving the scent of puppy breath
on my face.

I too am a piece
of God's nature
that he selected
to be here.
I decorate the world with my being
when I walk,
when I talk,
when I laugh,
when I cry,
when I scream.

Just being alive
buys me a ticket
to be a part of this graceful

moving landscape
passing by on a train.

I see the
beautiful movements
of a scrappy homeless woman
who's been discarded,
but who can still laugh,
and does,
and a child who's a little homely
and doesn't know it,
and skips gaily,
with arms swinging wildly.

We chose to be here
a long time ago,
and here
we are,
until we're not.

And when we're not,
we will be part of
another wildly beautiful landscape
not far from here,
or very far from here.

Perhaps a different landscape,
with a sky in green,
an ocean of purple,
puppies whose tongues are rough,
and kittens whose tongues are soft.
Different, perhaps,
but still
wildly beautiful.

MADNESS

It's good to let
madness out
once in a while,
to exercise it
and let it play.

Dance naked.
Laugh too loud.
Say something
inappropriate
to appropriate people.

Love bigger than expected.

MINE

Sometimes, a summer night's breeze
blows sweetly
just on me.

Sometimes, the night birds sing
their serenade
just for me.

Sometimes, distant music
from an outdoor concert
wafts by,
looking for me
and finds me.

Some nights,
a bright misshapen moon
smiles at me,
then throws moonlight
on me.

Some nights,

silver starlight
finds me
and sings a star song
to me.

Some summer nights
are just
for you.

This one
is mine.

MORE

Spend yourself.
You will not
go empty.

You will
get more.

MANMADE

"Manmade"
gets a bad rap.

Okay, so toupees are manmade.
And let's don't forget pink foil artificial Christmas trees.

But, so was
Vivaldi's "The Four Seasons,"
Beethoven's "Emperor Concerto,"
Da Vinci's Sistine Chapel,
penicillin,
red fingernail polish,
and cover-the-gray hair coloring.

And, in a way,
you and me.

VISIBLE WIND

I saw a little boy
in the park
trying to make the wind
visible
with a kite.
The kite blew about
wildly.

I thought about
how we try to make
feelings
visible with words,
and much of the time
about as accurately
as a kite
blowing freely
in the wind.

THE TRADER

They called her "The Trader." She collected emotions and, from
time to time, body noises. She traded these to people who were
looking for different emotions or body noises.

She collected sighs people had thrown away. She felt that too
many people dismissed their importance. She had a special fond-
ness for sighs and would trade them if she had to, but mostly
liked to keep them for herself.

Sometimes she would bump into someone who had laughs to
get rid of, as they had decided to indulge in a self-pity phase and
had no use for them. She gladly took them. Laughter was highly marketable. Polite, fake smiles were typically hard to come
by. People never knew when they might need them, and for
the most part, kept them for parties. Genuine smiles, however,

were easy to come by, as they were used much less and tended to clutter one's pockets.

The trader could get a lot of belches and farts from women as they were always anxious to off-load them. She supplemented her income quite nicely by selling them to teenage boys, who could never get enough body noises. When she had a fresh supply, she would motion to them through the chain-link fence at school and they would come running to her. Often, she would trade them belches and farts in exchange for joy, as they wanted to look cool, and everyone knows it's not cool for teenagers to show any signs of joy. She suspected that they secretly kept some of their joy, and shared it privately among themselves. They had made a secret pact however, not to show joy to adults, and certainly not to parents. They wanted to look gloomy and miserable at all times. Like the boys, teenage girls also liked to look gloomy and miserable, and would trade feelings of joy in exchange for pining, whining, and romantic notions. They also liked big, long, deep sighs which they used frequently while they dramatically rolled their eyes.

She noticed that all men, no matter what age, liked to trade for farts, especially after they were married. They'd trade any kind of sensitivity or tender feeling any day of the week for a good fart. Old men never sold or traded off their farts. They cherished them and used them profusely.

Dreams were either very hard or very easy to come by. Some people hung on tightly to their dreams and would never trade them. She noticed, however, a growing number of people who didn't believe in them anymore and would gladly trade them for feelings of resigned melancholy. Kids, on the other hand, always kept their dreams.

As she traveled the world, she noticed trends in trading. For example, feelings of sensuality were highest in France, actually quite high throughout all of Europe and surprisingly, Guam. Demand in the United States, however, was moderate to low, but only for men. Universally, there was a high demand for sensuality by all women, everywhere, all the time.

Children were willing to trade for any emotion, but reluctant to trade anything back. They even liked anger. They made no distinction between emotions, and played with anger with the same delight as they played with joy.

Hiccups were, by and large, easily obtained. And luckily, there was a small group that was very much into hiccups. No one really knows why. There was a large number of people who didn't see the need for rhythm, and would trade every bit of their rhythm for something else. You can see these people at popular dance clubs.

The Trader lived a happy life. She kept a surplus of all the emotions and body noises she collected, and enjoyed them in the evenings when there weren't any good shows on TV.

She loved her life and her profession. She never felt bored. She would call upon various feelings, depending on her mood and what she had in her closet. She was a happy woman and lived a rich, full life that was chock-full of a grand selection of lively emotions and magnificent body noises.

THE PALETTE

Yellow is nature's way of giggling.
Every yellow flower you see is a giggle.
Red is, of course, a hearty laugh.
Red has always been a bigger color.
Purple is the color of mystery.
All mysteries are shrouded in purple.
The word "calm" should never be written in anything other than blue ink.
I don't know why.

I Do

I do jealousy ... with great passion
I do hate ... ferociously.
I do sexuality ... succinctly.
I do love ... with precision.
I do insecurity ... as only an expert can.
I do envy ... with great hunger.
I do open ... when there's space.
I do closed ... when there's not.
I do passion ... when it doesn't scare anyone,
and sometimes when it does.
I do fear ... proudly.
I do sensuality ... in a slithery way.
I do rhythm ... when the music is good.
I do *hot* rhythm ... when I'm alone.
I do flying ... without a net.

Falling

When I fall,
I make it a point
to fall
up.

Falling down
is depressing,
and you can skin your knees.

Falling up is undoubtedly
more difficult
and it takes practice.

The only downside
to falling up is
if you're wearing a skirt
and no underwear.

To fall up
one must let go
of everything beneath the line
of what one thinks is possible.
This creates a vacuum,
and you fall up,
kind of like floating,
only faster.

Falling up is
uplifting.
It gives you
a feeling of lightness
and a rush of exhilaration.

We all fall.
That's unavoidable.
But when the falling rule was made,
it was not clearly stated as to
the direction of the falling
one must adhere to.

So, the next time
you find yourself falling,
fall up.

THE DREAM

I had a dream.

The dream
gave me a bird's-eye view
of the world
and its people.

From this distant,
higher view,
all the people
created one single,
beautiful, moving,
syncopated dance.

The rhythm of life flowed
through all of us.
We were dancing
to the same beat,
even though we were doing
different steps,
to give the dance life.

The people on the ground
thought
they were moving about
randomly
in massive chaos.

This was not true.

We thought
of ourselves as
bits
and
pieces.

None of us knew
how beautiful
we were
as a whole.

PRACTICAL JOKES

To whom
are practical jokes
practical?

DEPRESSION

Depression comes easily in fall and deep winter. It hibernates in spring and summer, as it can't stand the brightness of those days.

When depression first finds me, it comes upon me slowly as an opaque gray cloud. The cloud begins to cover me, growing on me like mold. If left untreated it becomes black and thick and sticky. This stickiness clings to me and is difficult to shake off.

Depression doesn't need a reason, and that is precisely what makes it hard to release. Sometimes, depression can come from being in sadness too long. Sadness is, however, different from depression, as it comes quickly, and usually has a clear reason for being there. Sadness can be silky and almost romantic. Depression is just icky.

Because of its insidious nature, depression is, at first, difficult to detect. It usually has a pretty good hold of me by the time I recognize it. It occupies me by taking my view of life and slowly and continuously turning it click by click, until I see life from an entirely different angle. A not-so-good, not-so-happy, angle. From this perspective it looks like my life has changed. It hasn't. Only my view of it has.

Hopelessness and despair are the colors that depression wears. It cloaks me in them like a suit of clothes. Joy becomes invisible.

I can only see joy's shadow. I can't touch it or remember what it feels like.

Just when I think all is lost, a little piece of joy taps me on the shoulder, lightly at first, then harder, and finally begins to scream out loud, demanding attention, demanding recognition. Finally, I see the little glimmer of joy. I grab it and hold on to it desperately, afraid it will fall into the muck below and be lost forever. It is so small.

But I need not fear, for the little joy is irrepressible and clings to me with strength and unwavering determination. And it begins to grow.

I start to participate in my recovery. I search for mechanisms of laughter and endorphin producers. I exercise, go to funny movies, go shopping—indulge myself in anything that makes me happy, anything that makes me laugh.

At first, laughter is forced. It is fake. Happiness is shallow. And then, suddenly, it begins to be real. I engage once again, with people, with friends. I start to share my feelings and as I do, depression is slowly released into the atmosphere.

As I actively argue with depression, God places quiet little miracles before me. I awaken to a day that is crisp and beautiful. A hummingbird comes to my window, suspended in flight, lingering longer than usual, looking at me. I smile. And it seems that he smiles back.

And so it begins, depression's demise. My true and right view of the world snaps back into position. The tiny particle of joy continues to grows, and expands until it is once again an integral part of me, living loudly in my life.

For joy, by nature, is stronger than depression, with a strength of will, a determination, that depression cannot ultimately suppress. And even though joy can hide from time to time, it will return in all its full glory. Depression is just a train stop, a skipped beat in joy's heart rhythm. Joy demands and shall have its rightful place as the core of all life and the essence of each beating heart.

Too

People used to tell me
I was
too sensitive,
too emotional,
too analytical.

Being too analytical,
I, of course,
analyzed this.
Here's what
I tell them now:

On a scale of 1 to 10,
I might be a
7 sensitive,
and you are perhaps a
5 sensitive.
So, as you see,
I'm not necessarily
"overly" sensitive.
You just may be
"under" sensitive.

Please feel free to use
this formula
if anyone calls you
"too" anything,
including, but not exclusive of,

too practical,
too spontaneous,
too logical,
too loud,
too quiet,
too shy,
too demanding,
and a multitude
of others.

THE STAIN

She hardly ever cried,
but finally one day,
she did.
And suddenly
she knew she was okay,
alive and feeling.

The tears carried
sadness toxins
up and out of her heart.

Sorrow, at last,
was flowing
in the right direction,
falling to the ground,
leaving a stain
where sorrow
had once been.

SALTY LIES

When you tell a lie
it feels coarse and rough
like a big piece of salt
coming up from
your throat,
scratching it.

When you tell
the absolute truth
from your heart,
it feels refreshing,
like drinking
a glass of cool water
on a hot day.

There are degrees
of truth and lies.
There are
"almost" lies,
and "partial" truths.
These feel like
something in between
salt and cool water.

The reason
we get these sensations
is so we can know
the difference.

I strive for cool water,
but often
find myself swimming
in a cool salty ocean.

HELL

Spending time
writing
is like spending time
with a lover.

Spending time
trying to get my book
published
is like jogging
in hell
wearing a tight, itchy, wool suit.

MUD HENS

On my walk in the park today
I saw a flock of mud hens
gliding on the lake
in perfect formation.

As they sliced
through the calm water,
symmetrical wakes
formed behind them,
and glistened
in the morning sun.

I was sure the mud hens
were not aware
of the beautiful scene
they created.

I wondered
if mud hens
look at us in the park,

having picnics,
playing with our children,
laughing,
riding on tandem bikes,
and think,
what a beautiful scene
we make.

NEEDED:

Gentleness.
That they don't look like
they need.
Please don't be fooled
by their tough exterior.

The toughest exterior needs
the most gentle touch,
as the soul it encases is so sensitive,
it needs
the protection
of a mighty fortress.
And so,
a fortress is built.

So,
the next time
you encounter
a strong fortress,
be very gentle.

This is especially true
with teenagers
with spiked hair,
black lips, and
tattoos.

These are merely
road signs to
"fortress up ahead,"
"easily hurt inside."

Please be kind
to these
gentle creatures.
They are
some of God's
favorites.

WONDERING

I often wonder, and yes, I do mean often, what restaurants do with the leftover bread from our tables, the part that's left after we've pulled our slices off.

The Health Department doesn't allow restaurants to put the remaining bread together with someone else's leftover bread and present it as "new bread" to a new customer. They're not allowed to give it to hungry homeless people—again, the Health Department. I never see them feeding it to the birds. Perhaps they're allowed to bread veal cutlets with it, but I doubt it. And anyway, how many veal cutlets can you serve in one night?

Perhaps the larger question is, why do I spend my time on such mental minutiae? I suppose it's to give my brain a rest from larger questions such as, "What is God's real name? How does He do what He does? And why?" Then, of course, there's the most perplexing question of all, "What do Mexican restaurants do with their leftover chips?"

FUN

In your own head
and in your own heart
is where all the fun happens.

Be there.

DOUBT

Doubt, doubt, oh hideous doubt.
Slithering darkness
permeating the light.
Snaking its way
into pastel moments.

Obsidian-colored
cousin to fear.
Darkener of the glow.

Tilt the scale.
Doubt the doubt.

What brilliance comes.
Shine forth light.
Obliterate the darkness,
taking light back
to its origin,
to the brightness
it longs
to be.

Glow on, glower.
Shine on, shiner.
Find the courage to be
blasted
by the brightness.

Bask in its warmth.
Be
all the brightness
you are.

ANNOYING

I don't understand
when someone says to me,
"I care about you."
It's such a
weightless thing to say.
A waste of words.
A waste of spit.
Devoid of substance.

I sense
the heavy avoidance
of the word "love."
Why?

People say they love:
their favorite ratty old T-shirt
a book,
a new car,
a song,
or a pair of comfy old shoes.
But they're afraid to use the word
"love"
with me?

STANDARDS

If you're not getting enough
of what you want,
raise your standards.
You'll get more.

Or,
lower your standards.
You'll find
you have everything
you want.

BORED

If you're bored,
go sit in the mall
and, as couples pass by,
imagine them
naked, making love.

If that doesn't do it,
imagine them
imagining you
naked, making love.

THE FUNNEL

One day as she sat on the rocks at a secluded beach, she happened
to look up and saw a dazzling light in the shape of a funnel. It
appeared to be coming out of the top of her head. She blinked
and the light was gone. She dismissed it, assuming it had been
just a trick of the sunlight.

The next day she went back to the beach. As she sat on the
rocks, looking at the crashing waves, she looked up and saw the

light again. She did this for six days, and for six days she saw the light. She noticed that when she was feeling open and happy, the funnel of light was open wide at the top. When she was feeling closed and not so happy, the funnel was closed.

On the sixth night she had a dream. A creature, looking suspiciously like an angel, came to her and told her that when human beings are born, the funnel of light is wide open, but as they grow and experience hurt, they learn to close it. She said that, often, the funnel becomes stuck in the "closed" position and will open only on special occasions. The creature/angel told her this was the opposite of how the funnel was designed to operate, and that the funnel should remain open wide at all times, and closed only on special occasions.

The next day when she went to the beach and saw the funnel of light, she began to play with it, opening it and closing it at will. She noticed that when the funnel was open, the feelings that came through were luminous and rich, and, well ... heavenly. When she closed the funnel, she felt tight and constricted.

From that day on, she kept her funnel open, closing it only on special occasions, as directed by the dream angel. She found she could still feel hurt, but by keeping the funnel open the hurt was captured by the light and flew up and away. Her life became radiant, and she felt a kind of unbridled joy that she hadn't felt since she was a child.

FLAWS

I have come
to be slightly
charmed
by my flaws.

Oh, yes,
I do recognize them.
And yes,
I do work on them.
But interestingly,
certain characteristics
considered "flaws" by some
are considered
"charming characteristics"
by others.

To some,
being outspoken
is a bad thing,
a flaw.
To others,
it's a good thing,
perceived as
honest, direct, and straightforward.

This makes it difficult
to determine
what my flaws
actually are,
at least by
other people's standards.

I, of course,
am not objective

about my flaws,
so I depend
on the viewpoints of others.

If everybody would get together
and agree on
what my flaws
actually are,
I'd be happy to change them,
but I think I'm safe
from that happening
for the moment.

And, I suspect,
forever.

Some Words

Some words
are more fun to say
than others.
Take the word,
"coconut."
If you're feeling sad,
just say,
"coconut."
You'll immediately
feel better.

Conversely,
never say
"snot"
when you're
nauseated,
or "blithering"

when you're drunk.
It won't come out right.

When you're feeling
heavy and
weighted down
with problems,
and your world
feels dark and gray,
just say
"bliss"
or "wind."
It'll lighten you right up.

Afraid

If you're afraid,
and it's a good thing to do,
do it afraid.

Sexist

The word
"sexist"
should refer to
someone who likes
and does sex a lot.

LOOKING AT DENIAL

I remember a time
when I stood
on just this side of denial.
I looked at it,
deciding whether
or not to step over
the line
and into it.

I needed a vacation
from truth,
just for a little while,
until I could
get my bearings.

I couldn't
afford truth
at that moment.
It was too big.

I needed it doled out
in little chunks.

After careful and
deliberate consideration,
I decided to step across
just for a short visit.

Before I crossed over,
I tied a rope
to truth
so I could pull myself back
at any time.

Although denial certainly has
its obvious benefits,

it's not a healthy place to visit
for too long.
It can suck you in
and keep you,
like quicksand.

So, into denial I went,
and there I stayed until
the time I could
afford truth
once again.

When that time came
I pulled myself back
and dealt with what was real.

I could then
handle it.

LOOKING AT A NERVOUS BREAKDOWN

I remember a time
when I was going through my divorce,
peering over the edge
at a nervous breakdown.

I could see the nervous breakdown.
I could touch it.

It looked tempting.
No blame.
No responsibility.
A rest for my mind.
A respite for my tattered heart.

As I stood, considering

the plunge,
I looked for a place
in sanity
to tether a rope
so I could come back
at any time.

But I noticed
that sanity
had no post
on which
to tie a rope.

I'd have to take my chances.

No.
Not without a rope.
Not without a guarantee
I could get back.

A person could get lost and
stuck there
forever.

I decided to stay
with my problems
and unravel them
bit by bit,
day by day.

A nervous breakdown
was too dangerous —
without a rope.

LOOKING AT ANGER, JOY, LAUGHTER, AND THE ORGASM

I don't ever remember a time
when I looked at anger
and contemplated
whether or not
to go into it.

There is no choice
or consideration.
I am just hurled into it.

For me,
there is no option
for anger.

The same holds true
for joy and laughter.
There is no decision to be made,
I just explode into them.

I hear it's that way
for men and their orgasms,
they are thrust into them.
There is no choice available.

As a woman, however,
I find I can stand
just on the border
of an orgasm
and decide
if I want to go into it
or not.

But then
I always do.
Why would anyone choose...
to not?

TO LEAN

I want:

The courage to let go,
fly free,
without even a dream
to hold on to.

To make everyone,
absolutely everyone
around me
an option, a bonus.
A marvelous option
and a spectacular bonus,
but nonetheless,
an option,
a bonus.

To not lean on anyone
to the extent
that if they leave,
I fall.
Stumble, yes.
Fall, no.

To stand as a blank canvas
and see what colors fill me.

To let the gods
fly me their way.
Not as a leaf
blown wildly by the wind,
but rather as a gull,
riding a current
that lifts me higher
and higher.

The courage to
let go of control,
to not direct.

The courage to lean on the wind.

RAINERS ON PARADE

There is a tribe of people called
the parade rainers.

The people who belong to this tribe
either had their parades
rained upon at a very early age
or were just born
wet, mean, and cranky.

These people think
raining on other people's parades
is a natural and good thing.

You can recognize them
by their dripping wetness.
They're cold, wet, and miserable.
They are not accompanied by parades,
as their parades have long since disbanded.
There's no music.
There's no marching.
There's no laughter.

Avoid this tribe at all costs.
They will drench your parade,
leaving you wet and chilled to the bone.

If you run into one of them
by accident,
put up your umbrella.

SPEED

She tried to be quiet, but even the sounds she silenced were loud. Her whispers roared. Her tiptoes thudded. She tried to blend in. She didn't. She tried to soften her edges, but her edges remained strong and bold. She tried to be pastel, but her primary colors screamed out loud. Her rhythm was just a heartbeat off from the rest of the world. She danced foreign steps to a tune nobody else heard.

She knew she was different. She didn't know why or how. She just knew her heart raced faster than the rest. At times, this difference felt charming and exotic, making her feel special. Mostly, it felt odd and alienating.

She had spent a good deal of her life trying to go slower. Think slower. Be slower. Be at the pace of the rest of the world. From time to time, quite by accident and without thinking, she let herself go and sped forward, enjoying the ride, exhilarated by the delirious speed.

One day, for no apparent reason, she decided to remove her self-imposed restraints and deliberately speed forward, allowing herself to go as fast as she could. As she raced at full throttle with her new unbridled freedom, she noticed others who began to zoom along beside her. She was surprised to have company.

As she gained speed, so did her companions. The wind in her wake sucked the others into her speed and they went even faster. They seemed to like it. Had they too spent their lives holding back their speed, lowering their voices, trying to be pastel, trying to fit in? Had they too felt different? Evidently.

For the first time, she felt the joy of racing at the speed that was her natural heartbeat. And she was grateful for the company of those who traveled beside her at the same lightning speed. The brotherhood and sisterhood she never knew she had.

To Be

I was either going to be a writer
or pretend to be a writer.

I opted to be a writer.
This meant
I would write.
I would write up.
I would write down.
I would write sideways.
I would write badly.
I would write well.
I would write.
I knew I might be a failed writer,
but nonetheless,
a writer.

It was my heart,
my soul,
me.

Heart pumping,
soul soaring,
me,
writing.

It was the thing
I could do
that was
the most opposite
of a sin.

A gift,
I hoped.

Not just for me,
but for others.

I hope
not just
for me.

FREE DAYS

There are strange and wonderful days that appear quite spontaneously in our lives, called "free" happy days. On these days the air smells sweet. Every movement is a joy and completely effortless. Your makeup looks radiant. Your hair glistens. You charm everyone you meet. Trees are greener. The sky is bluer. Lilting joy abounds.

There is no reason for everything to be going your way, it just does. You've done nothing especially right. You didn't do anything charitable. You weren't especially nice to the world. You just have free happiness. It found you, landed on you, surrounds you. You bathe in it. The world magically adjusts to your script.

Then, there are the "free" bad days. Again, no real reason. It's just so. It finds you, lands on you, and sticks to you. You haven't kicked any dogs. You weren't mean to old people or children. You just have a free, undeserved bad day. The air is thick, and even the slightest movement takes a great deal of effort.

It feels like your life hasn't changed, nothing has improved. The things that used to haunt you still do. The problems you've had in the past, you still have. It feels like you've made no progress whatsoever. You don't have a headache, but your head doesn't feel good. The word "malaise" comes to mind. The concept of joy sounds like something someone made up. Everything is a drag. The day shows itself in shades of gray. Primary colors fade. You feel listless. Everything is flat.

If you're having a free bad day, take heart, there's good news. These free bad days don't stay. And if you've used up enough free bad days, you're destined to come upon a free happy day, very, very soon. Through careful research and scientific observation, I've found that we get 3.5 times more free good days than bad days.

Dizzy

On our walk through life,
if we continually look down
we might find some money
lying on the ground.

If we look up, however,
we get to see the sky.

We can get dizzy looking up,
but it seems that
dizzy and the sky
are infinitely
a better choice.

Tears

Tears are exclamation points
for emotions that are too large
for the body to hold inside.

Tear ducts are
kind of like
overflow valves.

Happy or sad,
tears are simply
a form of punctuation.

The Left-Brain — Right-Brain Cha-Cha

It's a perpetual dilemma: to run wildly with the right brain, or move logically and precisely with the left. Some people have come up with a system depending on the time of day and day of the week. From nine A.M. to five P.M., Monday through Friday, they use the left brain. Any other time, such as evenings and weekends, they use the right.

Creativity resides in the right-brain, while the power to drive the creativity into action, and the detailed paperwork necessary to give creativity thrust, lies in the left. We love, of course, from the right brain, but I typically keep one foot in the left. That's probably not good, as wild abandon and hot sex can't happen unless one loves entirely from the right.

Dancing, singing and laughter come from the right brain. They make absolutely no sense, to the left. Balancing your checkbook is a left-brain activity. However, including an account column, called, "miscellaneous errors I could not find," is definitely a right brain function. Jogging in the park is left brain. Skipping in the park is right brain.

Most often, I find myself trying to balance squarely in the center, with equal access to both sides. It's a precarious balancing act, which I have a hard time doing well. I typically fall flatly into one side or the other. Then I overcorrect. Then I overcorrect the other way. The outcome is a ridiculous flip-flopping back and forth between the right and left brain, like a fan opening and closing.

I am not alone. I find that most of us spend a good deal of time in this same flip-flopping motion. Observing the flip-flopping is a left-brain function. Being amused at our never-ending attempts at finding balance is a right-brain activity and makes our right brain giggle.

THE MISTRESS OF THE
MEASURING OF THE DANCE

She was a trained specialist in measuring dancing. She was the "Mistress of the Measuring of the Dance." She had given herself this title. She knew it was long, but it sounded important, and she liked it. First, she'd measure the height and then the width of people's dances. She would then record the measurements in her "Dance Measurements" book. She had always felt strongly about her job, feeling she was performing a useful service in letting people know, should they ask, how their dance measurements compared to others'.

One day, she began to notice that people didn't seem too interested in the measurements of their dance. They were just enjoying the dance. She started to feel sad, when suddenly, the realization came to her that even though she had spent her life measuring dancing, she had never actually danced.

She decided to give it a try. She put on a red taffeta party dress, hung up her measuring tapes, played some lively music, and started to dance.

She doesn't measure dances anymore, she just dances. She dances wherever she goes. You can see her in town sometimes in her red taffeta party dress as she dances gaily to the dry cleaners.

HAPPY

Sometimes,
I'm so happy
I feel like I'm going to explode.

So, I calm myself down,
because exploding
is messy
and would make people
nervous.

RUNAWAY FEELINGS

There are runaway feelings floating about, looking for a place to
land. These fugitive feelings can be love, anger, fear, joy, jealousy, boredom, or just about anything. They can be good feelings
or bad feelings. They are not feelings we deserve. They don't
belong to us. They were lost by someone who wasn't through
with them, floated into the atmosphere, and are simply looking
for a place to land.

We do have a bit of control over these escaped feelings, and
can choose the ones we'll accept and the ones we won't. It
depends to some extent on the environment we present to
them.

Colors, for example, are magnets for a variety of feelings.
Black clothes can invite depression, but can also attract sophistication. Always wear a slight smile when you wear black, and
depression will slip right past you, allowing sophistication to
slither in.

Pastel colors are good for light, airy feelings like giddiness
and joy, but be careful, as superficial feelings are also attracted
to pastels. Try to be grounded and solidly true to yourself when
you wear pastel, and you'll attract joy and avoid superficiality
altogether.

If you get stuck with one of these fugitive feelings that's not to your liking, be patient, it will go away. It doesn't belong to you. It's just borrowing you for a time. For the most part, the feeling is just playing and won't stick to you very long.

ODD

I have become
odd.

And
I'm not old enough
or rich enough
to be considered
"delightfully eccentric."

To my mind,
I was always
a bit odd.
When I was young,
I tried to identify
the rules of oddity
so I could go the other way,
appearing to the outside world as
normal.

Now that I've learned to fit in,
I don't want to.
"Fit into what?"
I ask myself.
"To whose idea
of what's normal?"

Also, I've noticed
that I can be as odd as I want
and people make excuses for me

in their heads.
They change what they see
into comfortable explanations
for themselves.
They make
a round peg
fit comfortably
into a square hole.

I have learned
through practice
to dole out pieces of oddity
in precise, measured portions,
when I want
and to whom I want.

By this clever scheme
I am thought of as
interesting.
No one knows how
odd
I really am.

Except me.
And I have come
to honor it.

THE SMELL OF FEET

For two days, I had been smelling the smell of feet.

When I first noticed the smell, I bent down to smell my feet to see if that's where this odd, pungent odor was coming from. It wasn't. The smell continued into the next day and then into the next. Was it my body? Had my body started to smell like feet? Was it my new shampoo, my new makeup? No, after thoroughly checking out all of the above, I determined it was not. I considered that perhaps the inside of my nose smelled like feet. But then, how could I know?

I also considered that perhaps the world smelled like feet and always had. Only now, somehow, my senses were awakened and I was smelling the world as it really was. No, the world had always smelled just fine.

Then it came to me: I was smelling my life. My life had become stuffed into tight, sweaty places where air couldn't circulate. My life was cramped from being stuffed into small spaces. I had been stuck in the same place for too long. Same haircut, same clothes, same problems, same joys, same everything. My life smelled like feet. It stunk.

My eyes needed to see new sights. My brain needed to think new thoughts. My heart needed to beat in new rhythms. It was time for changes.

I thought about making a huge change, like moving to the south of France, but on further consideration decided I needed to make less dramatic changes than that. So, I went to the holiest of holy places, where I find solutions to life's most serious problems—the mall.

I bought a hundred-dollar bottle of the newest, trendy French perfume to get a solid jump on the feet smell. Then I went to the bookstore and bought a book on different religions, to broaden my horizons. At the stationery store, I bought a leather-bound journal with parchment paper, an Italian fountain pen with a white feather attached to the end, and emerald green ink. I would write every day in emerald green ink. At the food court, I saw a flyer on the bulletin board offering skydiving lessons. I took the flyer. I had always wanted to fly, or at least fall with control.

When I arrived home, a new smell wafted by me. It was the smell of gardenias, Spanish blood oranges, and a hint of some kind of sweet, peppery scent. The smell of feet was gone. The delicious new smell had replaced it.

This smell stayed with me for a couple of years, and whenever I noticed the slightest smell of feet creeping back, I invited new dimensions and new smells into my life. I never did do the skydiving, it was too scary, but I did eventually make it to the south of France — just a three-week vacation, but still, it smelled fabulous.

Chapter 5

TRIPPING THE
LIGHT FANTASTIC ~ GOD

This celestial dance has grand and glorious sweeping movements. It is the gentlest and most powerful of all dances. Danced throughout the world with different ethereal steps to different rhythms heard. And yet, it is the same dance, in the same ballroom, with a variety of tunes given to us by the same father... of dance.

Too big to be called by one name, feared by some, revered by others, adored by most, invisible power of goodness and light, a bright reflection of hope, joy, and all things possible. Called by many names, loved in many ways.

PAINTING

God gives us the colors.
We paint the pictures.
Sometimes,
we paint
with exquisite brushstrokes,
and our painting
is delicate and fine.

Other times,
we finger-paint
with bold, crude splashes of color,
and our painting
is unrefined
and yet,
oddly charming.

EVERYBODY

Some women get to wear Manolo Blahnik strappy sandals
from Rodeo Drive. Some children get to walk barefoot on
dry powdered earth because they have no shoes.
Everybody gets the sky.
The sky, sharp blue with whipped-cream clouds, or crystalline
blue and naked of clouds, or stormy and wild, bringing drama,
mystery, and wonder.

Everybody gets the sky.

Some people get to choose from a cornucopia of delicious
foods and luscious desserts to feast on every day. Some people
get to have a bowl of rice, and see it as a banquet.
Everybody gets the moon.
The moon, with its changing moods, displaying itself in a
kaleidoscope of temperaments, from a crescent sliver of

platinum to shamelessly full and round and glowing bold, and bright.

Everybody gets the moon.

Some people have never known war in their land. Some people have never known peace in their land.
Everybody gets the sunset.
The sunset in its explosion of colors splashed across the sky's canvas. Showing off in bold brushstrokes of crimson, which melt into deep orange and sign off in gentle strokes of apricot.

Everybody gets the sunset.

Some women get to wear slick Paris fashions and exorbitant jewelry. Some women get to wear rags and are grateful for them.
Everybody gets morning.
The crisp beginning of the day, when the sun is new, inviting fresh hopes and the possibility of delectable opportunities and grand miracles.

Everybody gets morning.

Some people get to be beautiful, and the world seems to grant their every desire. Some people get to be plain and are much ignored.
Everybody gets the air to breathe.
Air, sweet and delicious, carrying the fragrance of exotic flowers, freshly cut grass, the salty scent of an ocean breeze, or clean, fresh oxygen exhaled by the breath of trees.

Everybody gets the air.

Some people get to read books, allowing them to fly away to far off places, propelled by the words on a page and their own imaginations. They can choose from a wide assortment of books from bookstores on every street corner. Some people can't read and there are no bookstores.

Everybody gets laughter.
Hearty, sidesplitting, riotous, rowdy laughter.

Everybody gets laughter.

Some people get to have televisions, computers, cell phones,
microwaves, and every technological wonder known to
mankind. Some people have never seen a telephone.
Everybody gets to kiss.
A tender kiss from a mother, a wild, passionate kiss from a lover
or a sweet kiss planted on a puppy's nose.

Everybody gets to kiss.

Some people get freedom. Some people get political prison.
Everybody gets to think.
To play freely in their minds with great philosophical concepts,
to indulge in wild flights of fantasy and imaginative delights, to
create new mathematical formulas, or roll around in soothing
thoughts of cool ocean breezes.

Everybody gets to think.

Some people get health. Some people get disease.
Everybody gets dreams in the night.
Dreams, where all things are equal, and all potential for beauty,
wonder, health, and love exists, and where even people who are
crippled ... can run.

Everybody gets dreams.

And everybody gets ... God.

CONFUSED

It's been said
that God never gives us more
than we can handle.

He must have me
confused
with someone else.

THE CRUSH

When I crush an ant or spider,
or any insect
that has found me
in a foul mood,
or scared me,
I apologize
as my foot
comes crashing down,
saying,
"I'm sorry."

I wonder,
when my time comes,
from cancer or a car accident,
or whatever form of catastrophe
is destined
to crush my existence,
if I will,
at the very moment of impact,
hear a thundering
"I'm sorry."

SPLENDID

Most days
I see the world
through my dull brown eyes.

Every so often,
in a rare and wondrous moment,
I see the world
through God's eyes.

It's splendid,
and I cry.

God did not
give us
the words to describe
the absolute
splendor
of that
moment.

A PRAYER FOR MONEY

Dear God,

I need some money. Free money. I know it's not the
most important thing in the world. I know it's just
another form of energy, but it's a form of energy I
need. I want to live in a beautiful mansion. I want a
really cool car with a seat belt that's not shredding and
upholstery that doesn't have stuffing popping out. I
want to go on a vacation that does not involve a tent.
I have great things to do that require money. I want to
write more books. If I had free money, my talents
would have time to come out and play. I wouldn't have

to go to work. I could just spend my day writing, or maybe playing tennis, or painting.

As you know, I'm deep in debt. Home equity line debt, which I actually thought was free money. I want to get out of the hole and into the light. The money light. You've given me some good, hard lessons in life, and now, hopefully, I've paid my dues. I don't feel I need any more hardships. I think I have learned my lessons well enough. Can I just coast for a bit?

For the method of delivery, I was thinking that the lottery would be a good vehicle. Publishers Clearinghouse would also be fine. I don't want "death" money, however. No one should die. I also don't want to sue anybody. The money should not hurt anyone and it should be effortless. I could get a really big client that doesn't take a lot of work. I could find oil on my property. I could even find mobster money, but I don't want anyone chasing me. Someone could see me on the street and just like me. They'd be rich and give me a bunch of money just for who I am.

I would like to feel a free ride. A surprise bonus for nothing. A glittery, golden burst of sun on a cloudy day. I want to be showered in a rainbow of money. Is it my turn? Do people get turns? Do some get more turns than others? Do you have some free surprise packages lying around in your closet? Do you have closets?

I promise I'll be good. Well, I've been good. I'll be better. Just think about it.

Sincerely,

Carmen

P.S. And if for some reason I can't have the money, can I have a French accent?

THE CLUB

Besides God and angels,
people
are the most powerful
and most beautiful
creatures I know.

I'm proud to be in the club.

PONDERING

One day,
while pondering the question of God,
and trying to understand Him
and His ways,
I realized that…

If I think I can *understand* God,
I am either underestimating God
or overestimating my brain.
The bigness of God cannot fit,
in its entirety,
into my little brain.

If, however, from time to time,
I *feel* God,
well, that's entirely possible.
For the heart
is expandable beyond measure,
like God,
and there
He can fit.

MEMO TO GOD

Dear God,

I'm not trying to be a tattletale, but in case you haven't noticed, everyone down here is fighting about your name. "Jesus," "Buddha," "Allah," "Muhammad," "God Consciousness," "Higher Self," "Ganesh," "Shiva"—the list goes on. Please tell them what your real name is, so we can get on with more important things, like loving you and loving each other.

Even people who agree on your name, like Christians, have problems agreeing on your specific viewpoints. They come up with different interpretations from the thick book you left down here, and argue about them. People around the world are misbehaving, killing each other and indulging in unholy acts in wars they call "holy" for lands they call "holy." They seem to be confused.

If your intention is to have all of us love you, each in a unique and personal way, whereby all our love would come to you in a multitude of colors, so you can feel the whole of it in a kind of glorious rainbow effect, please tell them.

And tell them ... your name.

Thank you,

Carmen

STRONG SUSPICION

I strongly suspect
that when we die,
and get to know
everything,

we will find
that the kindest thoughts
we had about mankind
and ourselves
will have turned out
to be true.

A Prayer to God

Dear God,

Please let me find
someone to love
who will love me
as my dog loves me.

He loves me unconditionally.
He loves me for who I truly am.

He loves me
if I'm fat or old or ugly.

He doesn't care if I'm poor.
He doesn't care if I'm PMS-ing
and having a cranky day.

He loves me when I'm sick,
and even when I don't have time to
walk him in the park.

He loves me always
and forever.

God, please
let me find someone
who loves me
as my dog loves me.

ANOTHER PRAYER TO GOD

Dear God,

Please let me love others
as I love my dog.

Let me love them unconditionally.
Let me love them for who they truly are.

Let me love them
if they get fat or old or ugly.

Let me love them if they're poor,
or PMS-ing
and having a cranky day.

Let me love them when they're sick
and even when
they don't have time for me.

Let me love them always
and forever.

God, please
let me love others
as I love my dog.

ONE MORE

Dear God,

Let me love myself as You love me.
Let me love others as You love them.

And let my dog
go to Heaven.
Because if he doesn't go,
I'm not going.

THE BUG STEPPERS

There are three basic categories of bug steppers: The first group includes people who see a bug and go out of their way to step on it. The second group consists of people who see a bug and avoid stepping on it. The third group is composed of people who don't even see bugs or give them a thought one way or the other. Sometimes they step on them, sometimes they don't. It just depends on the luck of the bug.

The first group, the deliberate bug steppers, includes adolescent boys who are playing with their newfound power. It can also include people who are just having a bad day or people who are just mean. The second group, the non-bug steppers, includes Buddhists, who honor all life, even of the smallest order, plus especially kind and especially good people. The accidental steppers, the third group, aren't even aware that they're doing anything particularly right or wrong, and really they're not — they don't notice the bugs at all. I venture to guess, if a poll were taken, we'd find most of the populace to be in the third group, simply unaware.

I'm usually in the second group. I go out of my way not to step on bugs. I am ashamed to say, however, that in the past, on an occasional bad day, I have stepped on a bug or two on purpose. I now strive to honor and respect all living things, including bugs.

I believe God ... lives in the details.

GOD AND HIS SALES REPS

God is a marketing genius.

A long time ago, He sent some of His boys down to different parts of the world at different times, as His sales representatives. They were sent as "living visual aids" to remind us that He's here, He loves us, and we should love each other.

God assigned His sales reps to specific territories according to each rep's particular talents, abilities, and specialized sales techniques. He then sent them to their designated territories throughout the world, where He knew each one would have the most influence. Buddha was assigned to the Far East. He had specialized presentation skills that would allow him to successfully deliver God's message to people that lived there. (Buddha was also Asian.) Jesus was sent to Jerusalem because God knew His specific abilities would work well with people in that part of the world. (And, Jesus spoke Hebrew.) Muhammad, of course, was chosen for the Middle East. God knew that Muhammad could best represent Him and His message in those lands. (Plus, Muhammad could stand the dry desert heat.)

Assistants to the sales reps were also sent to help with the workload. These included saints, disciples, prophets, and some just really good people like Gandhi and Mother Teresa. They were the backup team, the support staff. The sales representatives and their assistants were sent by God to give us His words, His thoughts, His heart … to all parts of the world. It was a good plan.

All seemed to be going quite well and according to plan until, religions started to spring up … in the name of the sales reps. Christianity, Buddhism, Islam, Judaism, Hinduism. After a time, spin-offs from the main branches began to appear. Christianity split into Catholics, Protestants, Born-Again-Christians, Mormons, Jehovah's Witnesses, etc. The same thing happened with the other religions. And each of these sects was further divided into extreme and liberal factions. The people of the various religions started to war against each other, saying their sales rep was the only "Authorized" sales rep.

No one seemed to notice that all the religions had been given the same basic God-beliefs: Don't kill. Don't steal. Don't lie. Love each other. No one paid attention to the *big* beliefs they had in common. Instead, they focused on the little differences.

Each religion had come up with different rituals, holidays, and ways to love God. The people of the religions felt that their holidays, their ways of loving God, were the only right ways. And everyone else was wrong.

The religions also had different God books. These were God's sales manuals. God had given different manuals to the different peoples of the world with slightly different wording, slightly different stories, in order to accommodate the particular cultural aspects of that particular part of the world at that particular time.

Again, all the books had the same basic truths that God was presenting to all people. But still there was fighting. The Bible-people fought with the Koran-people. People argued about the most minute details of their specific God book. Un-Godlike things began to escalate, with war, killing, intolerance, and hate. Love was lost to unimportant details. The big picture, the big message was lost. The message of LOVE.

No one noticed that every religion, in its own language, has only one name for "God." Everybody remained stuck on the biggest disagreement of all—Who is indeed God's "Authorized" sales rep?—never considering that he had sent several. And even though the sales reps have different names, they all work for the same CEO.

God is also a brilliant advertising strategist. He knows that all successful marketing plans are backed up by comprehensive advertising strategies. He knows that one such strategy is an advertising blitz, called "media mixing," whereby one sales message is presented in different formats and styles, through different media to different people … all with the same message.

~ TV commercials are specifically formatted to appeal to people who relate to "moving images" and watch television.

~ Newspaper ads are presented in bold graphics to impact people who relate to "still visual" messages.

~ Radio commercials are created for people who like music and listen to the radio.

~ Billboards are designed for people who are stuck in traffic and cranky.

Being the advertising genius that He is, God implemented media mixing on a grand scale, not through standard media techniques, but through His different sales rep which gave him worldwide market penetration. He did not want to miss a single person. He sent his message in a variety of formats through all His sales reps. Same message different formats. To everyone. For everyone.

It seems to me that we are messing up God's great marketing plan. I also believe that the part of Himself He implanted deep within each of us will prevail. I believe this part is stronger than our human frailties and that God and His true intentions will win. We will learn to pull together, and rejoice in all the bountiful beauty we have in common. And in the end, the unimportant differences will be just that. Unimportant.

LADY OF THE RED STAR

As I stand on the precipice, I can jump with all my force and perhaps fly, or I can scale down slowly, safely. I leap off ... and fly.

I fly higher than I have ever flown. I soar through moonlight, close to its source, where it's blinding and bright, where the air is thin, where gravity has no claim on me.

Moonlight lands on me, and drips thickly off my wings, like honey. I scream loudly, joyful in my flight. No one hears me. I am far from all the anyones and everyones below. The crowd is congealed beneath me and unaware of me.

My will, my freedom, my wish to go higher propel me with great power. The slightest thought of my wish thrusts me higher. The stars whisper for me to go higher yet. I heed them with a resounding trust I have never felt before. I obey at this strange and wondrous intersection of time and delightful madness. The moment hurls me, carrying me faster, further, higher. The glory of it steals my breath. I find, I do not need to breathe.

A distant red star beckons me. In the power of the same wanting, I speed even faster to this strange destination, this red star. As I approach, the star's desire and my own touch, then mate, becoming one. The red star is a reflective surface. It sucks me in then throws me back my own reflection. I see wonder ... beauty ... goodness. It is me, through God's eyes.

In this moment, I am joyful of every life event, every sorrow, every happiness, every fear, every cut that made me bleed, every piece of every experience that has brought me to this moment of seeing myself in this celestial light. In and through these new eyes, I look down and see the beauty, the magnificence, the splendor, of all the people of the mass below. It is a thing to behold, a thing that I carry with me now back on Earth. I have been shown my wings. And in the discovery of my wings, I have discovered, yours.

As I stroll among you, my wings are neatly tucked inside my coat. In my pocket I keep the knowing of you, the wonder of you, the glory of you. The way God sees you. And as I pass by you on the street, I touch you, gently brushing my wing against you, hoping to remind you ... of yours.

EINSTEIN

Einstein said,
"I want to know
God's thoughts,
the rest
are details."
He was a "thinking" man.

I am a "feeling" woman.
I want to know
God's heart,
the rest
are details.

Chapter 6

THE CHARLESTON ~
OLD-TIME DANCING

The dance of aging. The joys and sorrows that accompany it. Old powers lost, new powers found. A dance of adjusting, accepting, changing. Some of us still clutching and clinging desperately to the dances of youth in this youth-oriented culture, not going gracefully into that good night. Others accepting and reveling in their newfound wisdom and fresh joys, enjoying this new view of life from a different, perhaps more interesting angle. The dance is slower, but no less wonderful than the hasty dances of youth. And finally, we all genuflect to this beautiful gift of life in all its stages, seen through the eyes of all ages.

GOOSE BUMPS

I met an old man
at the beach.
His skin
was wrinkled,
like a road map
that had been folded
wrong
too many times.

He told me
that the object of life
was to have
as many goose bumps
as possible,
as often
as possible.

He said one should
devote one's life
to seeking
goose-bumping
experiences.

I envied his wrinkles
because I knew
they were there
from his skin
having stretched
up and down
so many times.

He'd had
a life
full
of goose bumps.

LIBRARY BOOKS

Library books
should have
reference numbers.
People shouldn't.
Forget your age.
Be who you are
without a number.

IF I KNEW

If I knew then
what I know now,
I wouldn't have had
as much fun.

WORRY

Where did I find
all these things
to worry about?

Where were
these oh-so-scary things
when I was twenty?
Were they hiding,
lying in wait,
to jump out at me,
when I got older?

Does this newfound worry
prevent
bad things
from happening?

No.
they still do.
Or don't.
Mostly,
don't.

I have changed nothing.
I just spend more time
and emotion
fretting.

Did I have less to lose
when I was twenty?
I don't think so.
At least,
nothing of
importance.

At twenty
I had more faith
in life
and in good outcomes.

My horoscope
recently said,
"Let go of that cliff
you're so desperately
clinging to,
and you'll fall
precisely
three inches."

I think I will.

TINA TURNER AT SIXTY

Concert, San Jose Arena, November 2000

Strong.
Sexy.
Vibrant.
Still dancing
with fire
and passion.

Thank you, Tina.
I am no longer
afraid
to be
sixty.

KNOW IT ALL

When I was in my
"know-it-all" twenties
it was fun to theorize
about the meaning
of life.

Now that I'm in my
"every-theory-has-been-shot-to-hell"
late forties,
it's fun
to not.

WOMEN OF THE MIDDLE AGES

"Middle age" refers to a range of ages: 42, 47, 55. One would assume that "middle" age would be the halfway point between birth and death. We know, of course, half of the equation, our birth. We don't, however, know when we're going to die. So, middle age varies. If I'm going to live to 100, 50 is my middle age. What do I call myself past 50, just "old"? I guess it doesn't really matter, after all it's just a word. Still…

For non-argument's sake, let's call middle age from age 40 to 60, with the assumption that we will live anywhere from 80 to 120. I'm middle-aged and 49, so I must live to 98.

The first thing I've noticed to have changed dramatically, and almost overnight, is my body. It's not exactly fat, but it is thickening in the trunk region at an alarming rate. I no longer have a waist. My legs are still reasonably thin (mostly the lower part), as are my arms (again, mostly the lower part) — my weight seems to be shifting upward.

To show my body to its best advantage, I've taken to wearing tight pants, showing my skinny legs. I wear these pants with bulky, oversized sweaters. This tricky strategy gives people the impression that the rest of my body is as thin as my legs and that I'm just wearing a bulky sweater, not a bulky body. I have noticed this trick being used by other women of the middle ages also. A lot of women.

Another popular trend with my tribe is to wear T-shirts that have shiny gold decorations, like gold sequins or gold foil writing. These gilded tops are usually in the brightest colors, including hot pink and screaming aqua. I've made a conscious decision to avoid this trend, being of the mind that it shows flagrant insecurity. These bright colors and flashes of blinding glitter make a woman look like a billboard, and seem to yell out that she no longer feels pretty and can only get attention by wearing loud, obnoxious colors.

Of course, I have the same insecurities as the rest of my tribe. I would just rather not yell mine out for the entire world to see. I would rather have them think that *I* think I'm still pretty, in the secret hope that I might trick them too into thinking it's true.

I remember reading in *Vogue* magazine that when a woman reaches 30, she doesn't care what other people think. Well, 30 came and went. I still cared. Damn. I figured I was the unlucky exception, destined to spend the rest of my life imprisoned in caring what other people thought of me. Fortunately, somewhere in my 40s, my caring did finally begin to wane, and now, in my late 40s, there remains just a slight but respectable sliver of concern about what others think of me. It is a beautiful thing. I heard a motivational tape that presented the concept "What you think of me is none of my business." Wow. I was full of delight when it finally happened to me.

So, all in all, given the pluses and minuses of being a woman of the middle ages, I'd say a bit of a thickened body is well worth the trade for the freedom of caring most what *I* think of me, instead of what others think of me. At last, it's none of my business.

SHOULD AND SHOULDN'T SYNCOPATION

In my mid-fifties,
I realized
that I had become
stuck
in a "should"
and "shouldn't"
syncopation.

My world had become
saturated
with "shoulds"
and "shouldn'ts."

It made me
and my life
stiff.

Life was no longer free flowing,
natural, or beautiful.
Spontaneity was gone.
Luster was lost.

"Should" and "shouldn't"
live in the past
or in the future.
They don't belong
to the
now.
I had sacrificed
now,
the richest of all places
to live.

After careful thought,
I decided that
"should" and "shouldn't"
were made-up words,
created by someone who was
depressing and sad,
and probably dressed badly.

There was no legitimacy
to the words or
the concept.

Things either
"did" happen
or "didn't" happen.
These became

my new words.
They have served
me well.

PINK

When I was young,
my favorite color was pink.

Now, I'm a grownup,
and everything
in my life is
beige.

When did this happen?

I think
I'll go paint something
pink.

FINE WINE

Through fermentation,
some old-er women
turn bitter,
like vinegar.

Other old-er women,
through the same process,
turn
to fine wine.

I feel I am too often
the former,
but I forever strive
to be the latter.

AMUSEMENT

When I was in my twenties,
I thought men and women
were the same,
and what differences
they had
came from their parents'
having given them either
dolls or trucks to play with.

Now, in my fifties, I have discovered
profound differences
between men and women,
far beyond
the toys
they were given to play with.

I look back
with amusement
at my original
silly notion.

I wonder
what silly notions
I have now,
that I will
look back at
with amusement
in my sixties.

I DIDN'T KNOW

When I was young
I didn't know — that people really do die.
I didn't know — that love could stop.

I didn't know — that one day I would check the "Head of
Household" box on my tax return.
I didn't know — that one day I would be the head of household
of what some people would consider a "broken" home.
I didn't know — that one day I really would be fifty.
I didn't know — that I would care.

I also didn't know
~ sometimes, when it rains and my hair frizzes, it looks kind of
   cute;
~ I would give birth to a beautiful child;
~ when love stopped, it could start again, with someone new;
~ there are great tax breaks for being the head of household;
~ "broken" home is *their* definition, not mine;
~ when people spoke badly about me, they were just talking
   about themselves;
~ being fifty would bring a new, beautiful kind of freedom;
~ or that flowers I planted in my garden so long ago, could bloom
   so big and smell so sweet.

WRINKLE CREAM

As she got older,
her skin became wrinkled.
Even wrinkle cream didn't work.
She knew
it was time
to put wrinkle cream
on her personality.

The skin was done;
the personality
can stay taut
and beautiful
forever.

KNOWING NOTHING

When I was young,
things looked bigger —
trees, bushes, flowers, and people.

As I grew bigger,
things grew smaller.

I thought
it was a question of height.
I was only partially right.

When I was young,
I had a higher attitude
toward everything,
a sense of wonder and awe,
a sense that
I didn't know everything,
or maybe
anything.

As I grew up,
my attitude grew down.
I knew everything.

Now I spend my days
trying
to know nothing
once again.

FEELING OLD

If you're feeling old,
just remember,
you'll never be
as young
as you are today.
So, enjoy the day.

And you young folks,
if you're feeling too young,
take heart,
you'll be
older
tomorrow.
So, enjoy the day.

THE DELIGHTS OF MENOPAUSE

Sor-r-r-r-ry, there are no delights in menopause. Those of you who are actually *in* menopause will have recognized this title as sarcasm. Those of you who have not yet reached menopause, I would love to give you grand hopes for a future filled with womanly wisdom and triumph over the aging process. Alas, in good conscience, I cannot. Menopause is delightful to the same extent that a root canal is delightful.

Women who say they're going to wear a luscious shade of purple when they're old are ... lying. When women get old, they choose to wear hideous, brightly colored neon T-shirts with the names of exotic foreign cities sprawled across the fronts in large metallic letters. Think in terms of a lime green T-shirt with a big silver BANGKOK scripted on the front. And then there's the ever-popular hot pink tee with PARIS scribbled in shiny gold letters.

Don't think you'll be dressing with any kind of fashion sense when you're old. You will seek out and wear anything that glitters.

Like a crow attracted to shiny objects, you'll find yourself drawn to clothes that "shimmer and glow." This comes as a means of deflecting attention from our changing bodies.

During the process of aging, weight, for no apparent reason, shifts and multiplies. It seems to come from thin air, "thin" being a misnomer, as there's nothing thinning about it. You won't eat more, you just get fat in the weirdest places. Your waist fills in, or rather fills out and disappears. Your trunk becomes square. Belts become obnoxious-looking decorations that mostly accentuate your square body and lack of a waist. Your legs might stay thin, which looks quite ridiculous on your square body, like toothpicks sticking out of a box. Some women's arms stay thin. Mine didn't. My brother calls them "granny" arms. Flabby flesh hangs down and flaps about grotesquely when I move my arms. If you're fat enough, they also get dimpled. I still have that to look forward to.

Regarding sex, depending on whether you're taking hormones or not, you'll either go entirely flat or get hot and sexy. I take hormones and experienced the latter. It's quite a juxtaposition to have the burning fires of passion sitting, very friendly-like, next to my embarrassment and shame over the new body I've acquired. Plus, of course, there's no man around for miles.

On the few occasions I stumble upon an actual date, I find myself wanting to rip my clothes off with an impassioned cry of, "Oh baby, take me!" Should nakedness occur, what actually comes screeching out of my mouth is, "No, wait—don't look at me!" A real mood damper. Understandably, I don't find the irony particularly amusing. I am not alone. My friends who are my age also don't feel attractive, unless of course, they are wearing their hot pink PARIS tees and are in complete, sweet denial.

Once in a while, on one of the denial days, we will readily accept the attention of a younger man who smiles at us, and who, I suspect, didn't get enough cuddling from his mommy, and thinks he's going to get it from us. And, of course, there's the possibility that he's curious about what it would be like to be with a box-body. Perhaps he's bored and simply yearns for a novelty, something new, something curiously bizarre. There is also, on occasion, a younger man to whom we throw a sweet, warm smile, who looks at us, makes a grotesque face, and laughs.

"Thank God there are men your age," you might think. No, not really. Most men my age have become beer-bellied mutations of their former selves: whose belts actually disappear beneath folds of belly flesh, or who have lost all their hair and sweep the few remaining strands around their heads to "trick" us into thinking they have hair. There are, however, a few good middle-aged men who are successful, suave, handsome and debonair. These men work out, have full heads of the most beautiful salt-and-pepper hair, and a sophisticated, confident air about them, knowing they are in great demand. The problem is ... *these men don't want us!* They want, and can get, younger women, mostly blonde, and always more shapely than God intended.

So, we don't have the same weapons to go into battle as we once did. We can compensate, find other talents, other charms. We find another "shtick." Some of us become funny, using humor as a compensation technique. Some will don the air of a sophisticated matron who isn't interested in men, dressing to the hilt in understated, expensive-label clothes. Believe me, I know some of these women, and their loins ache with a magnitude of stored-up passion that is scary. I'm confident that if one of them ever got mounted and had an orgasm, the world would implode from the sheer energy that's been trapped inside her, and probably suck the poor guy into a black hole.

Then, there are some who, like me, bounce from shtick to shtick, not having found quite the right one. I've always liked dancing. It's not really a shtick, I just like to dance. I dance as if I don't care that I'm old. I guess that's kind of a shtick. I try to use trendy new dance moves I've learned from my twenty-two-year-old son. He says I look ridiculous. I probably do. I try to dance sexy, I'm sure I look even more ridiculous. I flirt as I dance, looking pathetic in my screaming-denial behavior, taking on the appearance of a cartoon character. Yet, I continue to dance. I like to dance.

Then, there's the guilt. I've lived a good portion of my life rolling around in guilt. I was raised Catholic — that alone is a precursor to guilt. In menopause, it worsens. From time to time, I find myself in a rare moment where I'm happy. Invariably, out of nowhere, I realize that I'm feeling happy and quickly catch myself and think, "What should I be feeling guilty about? I'm sure there's something." Like a heat-seeking missile, I look for any guilt within striking distance. I have a particularly long-range capacity. "I don't work hard enough." "I'm snippy to cashiers and overbearing to waiters." "I spend too much money on shoes." "I'm mean to telephone solicitors." (Actually, I'm okay with that one.) And then there's guilt's second cousin, self-doubt. "I'm not pretty anymore." "My personality is abrasive." "I'm cranky and have lost my pink girly-ness." "And my home is tacky."

In our middle-agedness we also take on obsessive-compulsive behavior. There is a wide selection of these behaviors to choose from. Keeping the house clean is a popular one. I believe this to be a weak stab at the illusion of having control over our lives. I find myself straightening the folds of my living room curtains, many, many, many times a day. I remember watching my grandmother do this and thinking, "How weird." Now, even though I can't explain it, I somehow understand. I clean, I scrub, I Clorox, which is somewhat odd for me, as I've never been especially neat or clean, and the smell of Clorox makes me sick. Another popular compulsion is the tireless search for exactly the right haircut and exactly the right hair color. "If I can just get the right haircut and perfect color, I will be pretty again and the world will be, as it once was, my oyster." I believe this is another deflection technique, steering attention away from the box-body and onto the most marvelous cut and color the world has ever seen. Another popular obsession is collecting small animal figurines. It's usually bears, frogs, or pigs, but any kind of miniature animal will do. Our homes become filled with tiny statues of one particular kind of animal. I don't know why we do this.

One encouraging note is that when you're in menopause you'll probably have better jewelry. And if not better, certainly bigger. Most of us are more successful than we were in our twenties, and some of us have appropriated some cash from our ex-husbands, enjoying more spendable income. And, of course, there's the home equity line, which was designed, I'm sure, specifically for the purchase of jewelry. Remember, we are attracted to shiny things. Big, shiny things. That would be big stones on our fingers, big pearls to wear with our neon tees, big bangle bracelets for our wrists that clank loudly when we move — in general, just big jewelry. Another deflection technique.

Have I mentioned wrinkles? I first noticed wrinkles when I was taking out my contacts, using a hand mirror that was lying on the vanity. I put my face down and "Oh my God!" I thought the sagging flesh was going to fall onto the mirror. I swore to never be on top again. (If, that is, I'm ever blessed with the chance of having sex again.) The good news — yes, there is a little — is that this can be taken care of surgically, which I have not had the funds or the courage to do just yet. Even though face wrinkles get the most attention, trust me, wrinkles go everywhere. Body wrinkles, for example, are larger than face wrinkles and look more like crevices. Forget backless dresses. There are now crevices, yes, crevices, on your back. That which does not get crevices gets cellulite lumpy: the stomach, the thighs, to name a few. Everything gets wrinkles except the earlobes. They still look fine. (Whew!)

Now, if you feel that I've dragged you into a dark, scary place, take comfort, for while it is true that menopause does have its drawbacks, there is a bigger truth, which is, God is ultimately a fair guy. In His just and fair wisdom, He does offer a few upsides to menopause. On a cold day, hot flashes are quite nice. There are no more messy periods or fear of accidental pregnancy. Hormones have given me some balance and made my skin glow. I actually do think I've gained some wisdom, and it's interesting to focus on other parts of myself rather than just the external. Women seem to like me now. They didn't used to — perhaps I was competition. I guess now I'm not. That's not a bad thing. I have come to know other women as sweet and loving people. This had somehow escaped my attention before. And between moments of hormonal imbalances filled with insecurities, there are large blocks of time in which I feel grounded and wise, and young women come to me and ask for advice. They listen to me, and look at me as if I am wise. Maybe, just maybe, I am.

I also ponder the fact that growing old is infinitely better than the alternative. I hold life as a precious gift and am ever grateful that I have the privilege to be alive, be it in a young or old body. I went through hormonal changes when I was a teenager and thought I would go crazy. I didn't. I went through awkward body changes and survived. I came to accept the changes. I'm sure I will again. I have also come to realize that life never gets boring, as we fortunate ones who are still able to enjoy it can view it from many different angles, watching life's beautiful story unfold in its ever-changing landscape. I have had the consummate joy of viewing life from many different perspectives, many different ages. I don't want to be twenty. I already was. I'll let the twenty-year-olds be twenty. I have the grand privilege of ... being fifty-three.